say it with cake

say it with cake

EDD KIMBER

Celebrate with over 80 cakes, puddings, pies
and more from the original Boy Who Bakes

KYLE BOOKS

PHOTOGRAPHY BY GEORGIA GLYNN SMITH · DESIGN BY ANITA MANGAN

First published in Great Britain in 2012 by
Kyle Books
an imprint of Kyle Cathie Ltd.
23 Howland Street
London, W1T 4AY
general.enquiries@kylebooks.com
www.kylebooks.com

ISBN: 978-0-85783-097-5

Editor: Catharine Robertson
Designer: Anita Mangan
Photographer: Georgia Glynn Smith
Photographer's assistant: Sue Prescott
Food and props stylist: Anna Jones
Food stylist's assistants: Emily Ezekiel, Zoe Allen and Becky Bax
Copy editor: Jan Cutler
Proofreader: Jane Bamforth
Index: Helen Snaith
Production: Nic Jones and Gemma John

A Cataloguing In Publication record for this title is available from the
British Library.

Printed and bound in China by C&C Offset Printing Company Ltd.

contents

To Matt,
my wonderful
partner and
best friend

I love baking. I love it because you rarely bake for yourself. I
can't remember the last time I baked myself a cake and didn't
share it with someone else. There is something so satisfying in
seeing others enjoying what you have made. Baking is at its heart
a social activity, be it making a wedding cake or simply some
cookies to take into the office.

For me baking is about flavour first and foremost – looks come
second. There is nothing more satisfying than tucking into a slice
of freshly baked cake, but when you're serving it for a special
occasion it's even better when the finished product looks stunning.
I am not a natural cake decorator so I have designed all of these
recipes to look beautiful whilst being easy to achieve. If I can do
it, so can you!

Some of my earliest memories are of learning to bake with my mum
and enjoying the cakes at family parties or at Christmas time.
Many of the recipes that appear in this book are inspired by
those childhood memories. I can always remember the cakes I had
growing up and they hold a very special place in my heart. Ask
most people what birthday cakes they had when they were little and
they will probably remember. I hope that some of the recipes here
will become part of your family repertoire and help you to create
your own memories.

Happy Baking
Edd x

Useful Equipment

Baking Sheets

I prefer to use heavy-duty light coloured pans, which can be bought inexpensively from restaurant supply shops and some kitchenware shops. Dark and flimsy baking sheets tend to bake unevenly and brown the base of whatever is baking on them too fast, whereas heavy-duty light coloured pans usually bake nice and evenly. I prefer baking sheets to baking trays as they have a lip around the edge and can be used for multiple recipes.

Cake/Loaf Pans

In general I prefer to use light coloured bakeware, it is normally better quality and bakes cakes more evenly. For the recipes in this book you will need a variety of pans, the specific sizes are listed in each recipe. A good place to start is with a set of three 20cm pans, about 5cm deep.

Bundt Tins

There a few recipes in this book that use either a bundt or bundlette pan. I prefer those made by Nordicware but if you don't want to purchase extra tins all the recipes in this book can be baked in regular tins, you would just need to adjust the timings.

Cake Turntable

Whilst this isn't a necessity it does make the job of decorating cakes a lot easier. If you do decide to get one there is no need to splash out, the cheaper plastic models will work for everything in this book.

8

Cookie Cutters

Only a few of my recipes use cookie cutters and for that purpose a small set of plain round cutters in multiple sizes is the main thing you will need. There are also two recipes that use specially shaped cutters, shaped to look like wedding cakes and Christmas tree decorations. In general cookie cutters are very cheap and can often be purchased for as little as £1 each.

Electric Stand Mixer

I use my Kitchenaid almost every single day and it really makes baking so much more efficient and easy. If you do a lot of baking I can't recommend an electric mixer any more highly. If you prefer to make things by hand that is fine of course, but be aware recipes in this book have been tested using electric mixers, both stand and hand varieties, so may take longer to make.

Food Processor

I love my food processor as it makes certain jobs so much easier. Whilst not strictly required there are certain recipes that might be difficult to make without one.

Measuring Spoons

When a recipe calls for a teaspoon of baking powder it means a level teaspoon, which is an accurate 5ml measure. You can't get this accuracy with the teaspoon you use to make your cup of tea so invest a couple of pounds and get yourself a set of measuring spoons. Most supermarkets sell them these days.

9

Mixing Bowls

I prefer to use a set of Pyrex bowls for baking because they are cheap, heatproof and durable, just what you need for baking. I prefer not to use plastic as they tend to retain a film of fat even after being washed, especially bad when making meringue.

Offset Spatula

Other than a cake turntable this is the best thing I can suggest to make decorating your cakes easier. Spreading frosting across the tops and sides of cakes is much easier using one of these spatulas as it gives more control and lifts your hand an inch away from the cake making it easier to get a flat surface.

Piping Bags

These are invaluable for piping out macaron batter in perfect little rounds but are also useful for piping choux pastry or royal icing. I prefer to use the disposable type as it makes for much easier clean up.

Rolling Pin

This is a necessity for rolling out sugarpaste to cover your cakes. I prefer to use a large polythene model as it very smooth, which means smoother sugarpaste when rolling it out.

Sugar Thermometer

Where a recipe indicates that a sugar syrup needs to be cooked to a specific degree a sugar thermometer is needed to achieve this accuracy. I prefer to use a Thermapen, a quick-read digital probe thermometer

Wire racks

I never seem to have enough wire racks and it's only when you don't have any that you realise how useful these are. I would suggest a set of three should be all you really need.

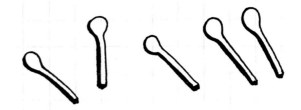

birthdays
& parties

Strawberry Shortcake

SERVES 12-15

butter, for greasing
5 **large eggs**
130g **caster sugar**
1 tsp **vanilla extract**
125g **plain flour**
30g **unsalted butter**,
  melted and cooled
1.2kg **strawberries**,
  hulled and quartered
icing sugar, for dusting

For the vanilla syrup
240g **caster sugar**
1 tsp **vanilla bean paste**

**For the vanilla
whipped cream**
500ml **double cream**
½ tsp **vanilla bean paste**
2 tsp **icing sugar**

What better cake could you serve during the summer, when strawberries are at their best, than this towering beauty? A light sponge is filled with freshly whipped cream, and lots and lots of strawberries – I can't think of anything better. The cake uses a genoise sponge, which is very easy to make, just follow the steps and you will have a wonderfully light cake.

1. Preheat the oven to 180°C (160°C fan oven) mark 4, then grease and line two 20cm cake tins with baking parchment, greasing the parchment too.

2. Put the eggs, sugar and vanilla into a heatproof bowl set over a pan of gently simmering water, making sure the bowl doesn't touch the water. Whisk constantly until the sugar has dissolved and the mixture is just warm to the touch. Remove the bowl from the pan and, using an electric mixer, whisk for 5 minutes on high speed, then reduce the speed to medium and whisk for a further 3 minutes. By this stage the mixture should have tripled in volume, and when the whisk is lifted from the bowl it should form a slowly dissolving ribbon.

3. Sift in the flour and gently fold together, making sure all the flour is combined, but trying to keep as much volume as possible. Take a large spoonful of the batter and add it to the melted butter, then mix together (this will lighten the butter and help to incorporate it into the batter). Gently fold this into the batter.

4. Divide the batter equally between the prepared tins and gently level out. Bake for 25 minutes or until risen and golden, or when a skewer inserted into the centre of the cake comes out clean. Allow the cakes to cool in the tins for 10 minutes before turning out onto a wire rack to cool completely.

5. To make the syrup, put the sugar and 240ml water into a small pan and bring to the boil, then simmer for a few minutes until the sugar has dissolved. Remove from the heat and stir in the vanilla paste.

6. To make the vanilla whipped cream, put the cream, vanilla and sugar into a large bowl and whisk until the cream forms soft peaks.

7. To assemble the cake, use a serrated knife to slice each cake into two layers and put the first layer on a cardboard cake board or serving plate. Brush with a generous amount of syrup and top with just under a quarter of the strawberries and a third of the whipped cream. Repeat with the other layers and top the finished cake with the remaining strawberries, dusting with a little icing sugar for decoration.

TIP

As this cake is filled with whipped cream, it is best served as soon as it is assembled.

Luscious Lemon Cake

SERVES 12

225g unsalted **butter**,
  at room temperature,
  plus extra for greasing
325g **plain flour**
50g **cornflour**
4½ tsp **baking powder**
½ tsp **salt**
400g **caster sugar**
2 tsp **vanilla extract**
4 medium **eggs**, separated
300ml **whole milk**

**For the lemon Italian
meringue buttercream**
250g **caster sugar**
6 medium **egg whites**
450g unsalted **butter**,
  at room temperature
200g **lemon curd**
yellow gel food colouring

This would be the perfect birthday cake for my mum. She loves lemon, and this cake is full of that gorgeous zesty lemon flavour. The bright frosting turns the cake into something a little more elegant – and don't worry, it's really easy to achieve.

1. Preheat the oven to 180°C (160°C fan oven) mark 4, then grease and line three 20cm round cake tins with baking parchment, greasing the parchment too. In a medium bowl whisk the flour, cornflour, baking powder and salt together to combine, then set aside. Put the butter into a large bowl and, using an electric mixer, beat on medium–high speed until smooth and light. Add the sugar and beat until light and fluffy, about 5 minutes.

2. Add the vanilla and mix to combine. With the mixer on medium speed, add the egg yolks, one at a time, beating until fully combined before adding the next. With the mixer on low, sift in the flour mixture in three additions, alternating with the milk, starting and finishing with the flour.

3. Put the egg whites into a clean, grease-free bowl and whisk until they hold soft peaks. Add the whites to the cake batter and gently fold together until just combined and there are no streaks of white.

4. Divide the batter evenly between the prepared tins and bake for 30–35 minutes or until the cakes are golden brown and spring back when lightly touched. Allow the cakes to cool in the tins for 10 minutes before turning out onto a wire rack to cool completely.

5. To make the buttercream, put 160ml water and the sugar into a pan over medium heat, and have a sugar thermometer ready. Put the egg whites into a clean, grease-free bowl (this is best done using a freestanding electric mixer). As the syrup reaches about 115°C, start whisking the whites on high speed. Cook until the syrup registers 121°C, then remove from the heat and, with the mixer still running, pour the syrup in a slow stream down the side of the bowl containing the whites, avoiding the beaters. Continue whisking on high speed until the meringue is at room temperature.

6. With the mixer on medium–high speed, add the butter, a few pieces at a time, beating until fully combined. When adding the butter it can sometimes look curdled; if this happens, don't worry, just keep mixing and eventually it will smooth out again forming a light buttercream. Add half the lemon curd and mix to combine.

7. To assemble the cake, put the first cake layer on a cardboard cake board or serving plate and top with a layer of the buttercream. Spread half the remaining lemon curd on top, leaving a 2cm border around the edge. Top with the second cake layer and repeat as before, then top with the last layer of cake.

8. To finish the cake, take a third of the remaining buttercream and add a little yellow food colouring so that there is a strong contrast between the two batches. Take the yellow buttercream and apply around the bottom third of the cake. This can either be done with a small offset spatula or a piping bag. Take the remaining buttercream and apply to the top and remaining two-thirds of the sides.

9. Using a spoon or spatula, draw a swirl pattern around the sides of the cake, this will slightly blend the two colours creating a beautiful gradient, like a sunset. Repeat the swirl on the top of the cake.

16

White Chocolate Rainbow Cake

SERVES 18

225g **unsalted butter**, at room temperature, plus extra for greasing
325g **plain flour**
50g **cornflour**
4½ tsp **baking powder**
½ tsp **salt**
400g **caster sugar**
2 tsp **vanilla extract**
4 medium **eggs**, lightly beaten
300ml **whole milk**

gel food colouring in **red, yellow, orange, purple, blue** and **green**

For the white chocolate Italian meringue frosting
150g **white chocolate**
300g **caster sugar**
6 medium **egg whites**
540g **unsalted butter**, at room temperature

This cake is a monster – it has six layers and uses a lot of butter, but do keep in mind that it will serve a lot of people, and it will make a spectacular cake for a birthday or any other occasion. The beauty of this cake is that, apart from being rather large, it looks quite innocent from the outside, because the white frosting hides the multicoloured rainbow inside. Imagine people's reactions when it is first cut into – it's well worth the effort.

1. Preheat the oven to 180°C (160°C fan oven) mark 4, then grease and line three 20cm round cake tins with baking parchment, greasing the parchment too. In a medium bowl, whisk the flour, cornflour, baking powder and salt together to combine, then set aside.

2. Put the butter into a large bowl and, using an electric mixer, beat on medium–high speed until smooth and light. Add the sugar and beat until light and fluffy, about 5 minutes, then add the vanilla and mix to combine. With the mixer on medium speed, add the egg yolks, one at a time, beating each until fully combined before adding the next. With the mixer on low, sift in the flour mixture in three additions, alternating with the milk, starting and finishing with the flour.

3. Put the egg whites into a clean, grease-free bowl and whisk until they hold soft peaks. Add the whites to the cake batter and gently fold together until just combined and there are no streaks of white. Divide the batter equally between six small bowls. Add a small amount of each colouring to each bowl, enough to make it a vibrant colour. Add the first three bowls to the prepared tins and bake for 15 minutes or until they spring back when lightly touched. Allow to cool in the tins for 10 minutes before turning out onto a wire rack to cool completely. Repeat with the remaining three portions of batter.

4. To make the frosting, melt the chocolate in a heatproof bowl set over a pan of gently simmering water, making sure the base of the bowl doesn't touch the water. Remove from the heat and allow to cool.

5. Put 190ml water and the sugar into a pan over medium heat. Bring to the boil and have a sugar thermometer ready. Meanwhile, put the egg whites into a clean, grease-free bowl (this is best done using a freestanding electric mixer). Start whisking the whites on high speed when the syrup in the pan reaches about 115°C on the sugar thermometer. Cook until the syrup registers 121°C. With the mixer still running, pour the syrup in a slow stream down the side of the bowl containing the whites, avoiding the beaters. Continue whisking on high speed until the meringue is at room temperature. With the mixer on medium–high speed, add the butter a few pieces at a time, beating until fully combined. When adding the butter it can sometimes look curdled; if this happens don't worry, just keep mixing and eventually it will smooth out to form a light buttercream frosting. With the mixer on medium speed, pour in the melted chocolate and mix until fully combined.

6. To assemble the cake, put the purple cake layer on a cardboard cake board or serving plate and top with a thin layer of frosting. Repeat the process with the other cake layers in the order of a rainbow (purple, blue, green, yellow, orange, red) and then spread the remaining frosting across the top and sides of the cake.

18

Tiramisu Charlotte

SERVES 15

25g **unsalted butter**, melted and cooled, plus extra butter for greasing
4 large **eggs**
100g **caster sugar**
100g **plain flour**

For the mascarpone mixture
4 large **eggs**, separated
150g **caster sugar**
250g **mascarpone**

For the coffee syrup
150ml strong **coffee**, preferably espresso
4 tbsp **Marsala** or **Madeira**, or to taste

To finish
cocoa powder, for dusting
200g **savoiardi biscuits**
100g **dark chocolate** (about 70% cocoa solids), in one piece

I absolutely love tiramisu – it's a dish I will almost always order in a good Italian restaurant, but it's not always the most attractive dessert in the world. My rather more elegant take on the traditional recipe is in the form of a charlotte, which makes it even more special and suitable for any occasion. To create an even prettier presentation, wrap the whole cake in a piece of ribbon.

1. Preheat the oven to 180°C (160°C fan oven) mark 4 fan, then grease and line a 20cm cake tin with baking parchment, greasing the parchment too. Put the eggs and sugar into a heatproof bowl set over a pan of gently simmering water, making sure the base of the bowl doesn't touch the water. Whisk constantly until the sugar has dissolved and the mixture is just warm to the touch.

2. Remove the bowl from the pan and, using an electric mixer, whisk for 5 minutes on high speed, then reduce the speed to medium and whisk for a further 3 minutes. By this stage the mixture should have tripled in volume, and when the whisk is lifted from the bowl it should form a slowly dissolving ribbon.

3. Sift in the flour and gently fold together, making sure all the flour is combined, but trying to keep as much volume as possible. Take a large spoonful of the batter and add it to the melted butter, then mix together (this will lighten the butter and help to incorporate it into the batter). Gently fold this into the batter.

4. Pour the batter into the prepared tin and gently level out. Bake for 25 minutes or until the cake is risen and golden, or when a skewer inserted into the middle of the cake comes out clean. Allow to cool in the tin for 10 minutes before turning out onto a wire rack to cool completely.

5. To make the mascarpone mixture, beat the egg yolks and 100g of the caster sugar until pale and creamy, then add the mascarpone and beat until smooth. Put the egg whites into a clean, grease-free bowl and whisk until they form soft peaks. Slowly add the remaining sugar and whisk to form firm peaks. Gently fold the meringue into the mascarpone mixture and set aside. To make the coffee syrup, mix the coffee and Marsala together in a small bowl.

6. To assemble the cake, use a serrated knife to slice the cake into three layers, then put the first layer into the base of a 23cm springform cake tin. Brush the top with about a third of the coffee syrup and top with just under half the mascarpone mixture. Dust the mascarpone with about 1 heaped tsp cocoa powder. Repeat the process with the second layer of cake.

7. Press the savoiardi biscuits down around the sides of the tin, then add the final layer of cake to the top and gently press down (this will help to stick the biscuits to the cake). Brush with the coffee and top with the remaining mascarpone mixture, gently levelling it out. Chill the cake for 4 hours. Just before serving, use a sharp knife or a vegetable peeler to grate the bar of chocolate to create shavings. Top the cake with the chocolate shavings, then remove the springform collar.

21

Candy Bar Cake

SERVES 12

225g **unsalted butter**, at room temperature, plus extra for greasing	**For the caramel** 100g **caster sugar**
325g **plain flour**	⅛ tsp **flaked sea salt**
50g **malt powder** (such as Ovaltine)	100ml **double cream**
4½ tsp **baking powder**	5g **unsalted butter**
½ tsp **salt**	
400g **caster sugar**	**For the whipped**
2 tsp **vanilla extract**	**ganache frosting**
5 medium **egg whites**, lightly beaten	450g dark chocolate (about 70% cocoa solids), finely chopped
300ml **buttermilk**	450g double cream

Everyone loves a candy bar – what's your favourite? When I was little I would either go for a Snickers or a Mars bar and it is the latter that inspired this cake. The cake layers are intended to be the malt nougat, and then you have a caramel filling and a chocolate frosting just like the candy bar. If you want to make a cake that's a bit more like a Snickers bar, add some crushed peanuts in between each layer.

1. Preheat the oven to 180°C (160°C fan oven) mark 4, then grease three 20cm round cake tins with baking parchment, greasing the parchment too. In a medium bowl whisk the flour, malt powder, baking powder and salt together to combine, then set aside.

2. Put the butter into a large bowl and, using an electric mixer, beat on medium–high speed until smooth and light, add the sugar and beat until light and fluffy, about 5 minutes. Add the vanilla and mix to combine.

3. With the mixer on medium speed, add the egg whites a little at a time, beating until fully combined before adding more. With the mixer on low, sift in the flour mixture in three additions, alternating with the buttermilk, starting and finishing with the flour.

4. Divide the batter between the prepared tins and bake for 25–30 minutes or until the cakes spring back when lightly touched. Allow the cakes to cool in the tins for 10 minutes before turning out onto a wire rack to cool completely.

5. To make the caramel, put the sugar into a medium pan and dissolve over medium heat until dark golden brown in colour, stopping before it starts to smoke. Remove from the heat and carefully pour in the salt and half the cream. The mixture will bubble violently, so be careful and go slowly.

6. Once the mixture has settled, add the remaining cream followed by the butter. If the mixture is lumpy, put back on the heat and stir until smooth. Pour into a glass jug to cool while you make the frosting.

7. To make the ganache frosting, put the chocolate into a large heatproof bowl and set aside. Pour the cream into a medium pan and bring to the boil. Pour the cream over the chocolate and leave for a few minutes before gently stirring together to form a silky smooth ganache. Allow the ganache to cool to room temperature (about 2 hours) and then whisk until light and thickened – be careful, because if you over-whisk the ganache it can become grainy.

8. To assemble the cake, put the first cake layer on a cardboard cake board or serving plate. Spread a quarter of the frosting onto the cake and top with a layer of caramel, leaving a 1–2cm border. Repeat with the second cake layer and top with the final cake layer. Spread the remaining frosting across the top and sides of the cake.

Classic Birthday Cake

Everyone remembers the birthday cakes of their childhood, and this is my version of the cake that many people will have eaten countless times. It's a simple cake covered in a super-easy chocolate frosting, for that taste of nostalgia - nothing fancy but super-delicious.

1. Preheat the oven to 180°C (160°C fan oven) mark 4, then grease and line three 20cm cake tins with baking parchment, greasing the parchment too. In a medium bowl whisk the flour, baking powder and salt together to combine, then set aside.

2. Put the butter into a large bowl and, using an electric mixer, beat on medium–high speed until smooth and light. Add the sugar and beat until light and fluffy, about 5 minutes, then add the vanilla and mix to combine.

3. With the mixer on medium speed, add the eggs, a little at a time, beating until fully combined before adding more. With the mixer on low, sift in the flour mixture alternating with the milk, in three additions starting and finishing with the flour.

4. Divide the batter evenly among the prepared tins and bake for 25–30 minutes or until the cakes spring back when lightly touched. Allow to cool in the tins for 10 minutes before turning out onto a wire rack to cool completely.

5. To make the frosting, melt the chocolate in a heatproof bowl set over a pan of gently simmering water, making sure the base of the bowl doesn't touch the water. Remove from the heat and allow to cool slightly.

6. Put the butter, icing sugar and salt in the bowl of a food processor and process until the mixture is smooth and light (Alternatively, beat together in a large bowl with an electric whisk.) Pour in the chocolate and cream, and pulse or briefly whisk to combine.

7. To assemble the cake, put the first cake layer on a cardboard cake board or serving plate. Put a large spoonful of the frosting on the cake and spread it evenly over the top. Repeat with the second layer, and then top with the final layer of cake. Spread the remaining frosting over the top and sides of the cake.

ME AND MY TWIN BROTHER SIMON

Lemon Present Cake

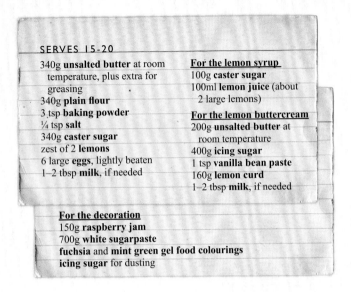

SERVES 15-20

340g **unsalted butter** at room temperature, plus extra for greasing
340g **plain flour**
3 tsp **baking powder**
¼ tsp **salt**
340g **caster sugar**
zest of 2 **lemons**
6 large **eggs**, lightly beaten
1–2 tbsp **milk**, if needed

For the lemon syrup
100g **caster sugar**
100ml **lemon juice** (about 2 large lemons)

For the lemon buttercream
200g **unsalted butter** at room temperature
400g **icing sugar**
1 tsp **vanilla bean paste**
160g **lemon curd**
1–2 tbsp **milk**, if needed

For the decoration
150g **raspberry jam**
700g **white sugarpaste**
fuchsia and **mint green gel food colourings**
icing sugar for dusting

A cake decorated to look like a present makes a fun birthday surprise. The cake and the decoration are simple to make yet the cake is striking in appearance with its lovely large bow. If you want to take the decoration a bit further you can use any leftover sugarpaste to cut out dots, and then stick these to the cake to look like patterned wrapping paper.

1. Preheat the oven to 180°C (160°C fan oven) mark 4, then grease and line a 20cm square cake tin with baking parchment. In a medium bowl sift together the flour, baking powder and salt, then set aside.

2. Put the butter, sugar and lemon zest into a large bowl and, using an electric mixer, beat on medium–high speed until light and fluffy, about 5 minutes. Add the eggs, a little at a time, beating well between each addition. Once fully combined, add the flour mixture in three additions, mixing until just combined. If the batter feels a little stiff, add 1–2 tbsp milk to lighten it.

3. Pour the batter into the prepared tin and gently level out. Bake for about 1¼ hours or until a skewer inserted into the centre of the cake comes out clean. If the cake is browning too quickly, put a tent of foil over the top. Allow the cake to cool in the tin for 15 minutes before turning out onto a wire rack to cool completely. If the cake is domed, use a serrated knife to level it.

4. To make the lemon syrup, put the sugar and lemon juice into a small pan and bring just to the boil, then gently simmer to dissolve the sugar. Remove from the heat and set aside until needed.

5. To make the buttercream, put the butter into a large bowl and, using an electric mixer, beat until lightened and smooth, about 3 minutes. Slowly add the icing sugar to the butter, beating until incorporated, then beat on high speed for a few minutes until the buttercream is light and fluffy. Add the lemon curd and beat until combined. If the buttercream feels a little stiff, add 1–2 tbsp milk to lighten it.

6. To assemble the cake, turn the cake upside down and slice into two even layers. Put the first cake layer (that was the top) onto a square cardboard cake board and brush the cake with a good soaking of lemon syrup. Spread the jam evenly across the cake, leaving a 1–2cm border. Top with a layer of buttercream and then with the second layer of cake. Brush with more of the lemon syrup, and then cover the whole cake with the remaining buttercream. Allow the buttercream to set for 15 minutes before covering with the sugarpaste.

7. Take two-thirds of the white sugarpaste and knead it until pliable. The colder the sugarpaste the longer it will need to be worked with to soften it. Dip a cocktail stick into the mint green colouring, add to the sugarpaste and knead until evenly combined. Dust the work surface with icing sugar. Using a large rolling pin, roll the sugarpaste into a square about 3–4mm thick and large enough to cover the top and sides of the cake. The easiest way to do this is to take a piece of string and use it as a guide. Drape it over the cake and grip it where it meets the table. Lift the string from the cake and use this as a measure for your sugarpaste.

24

8. Using the flats of your hands and arms to support the sugarpaste, gently drape the sugarpaste over the cake, and smooth the top with your hands, applying a gentle pressure. Carefully work your way around the cake, gently smoothing the sugarpaste onto the sides until you have a smooth square cake, trimming off the excess. Set the cake aside.

9. Take the remaining white sugarpaste and knead it until pliable then add a small amount of fuschia colouring to the centre and knead until evenly combined. Roll out the sugarpaste into a long rectangle about 3mm thick. Cut out three ribbons, two about 30cm in length and 3cm wide and one 25cm in length and 3cm wide. Take the longer ribbons and brush the underside with a little water, to act as a glue, then stick them to the cake to form a cross to look like a wrapped present.

10. To form the ribbon, cut the third length of sugarpaste into two even pieces and fold them over to form two loops, pressing them to seal together. Take the ends of the loops and gently squeeze in the centre to form a pleat. Using a little water, glue the ribbons together and then allow these loops to dry for at least 1 hour so that they hold their shape. Once dried, use a short length of sugarpaste 3cm wide to wrap around the centre of the bow to cover the join, and then put the bow onto the cake. You can leave the bow as it is or you can add tails to the ribbon by cutting out two more short lengths, 3cm wide, then cutting out a V-shape on both pieces and putting them under the bow.

Simple Celebration Chocolate Cake

SERVES 12

30g cocoa powder
50ml strong hot **coffee**
50ml hot **water**
200g **unsalted butter**
200g **dark chocolate** (about 70% cocoa solids), finely chopped
300g **soft light brown sugar**
4 large **eggs**
175g **self-raising flour**
1 tsp **baking powder**

For the chocolate buttercream
100g **dark chocolate** (about 70% cocoa solids), finely chopped
175g **unsalted butter** at room temperature
75ml **double cream**
375g **icing sugar**
a pinch of **salt**

For the decoration
500g **white sugarpaste**
icing sugar, for dusting
200g **coloured sugarpaste**

I've made this easy, but richly flavoured, cake to be a blank canvas for your decorative imagination. My version is made to look like a cake from a cartoon, but you can decorate it however you fancy.

1. Preheat the oven to 180°C (160°C fan oven) mark 4, then grease and line two 20cm cake tins with baking parchment, greasing the parchment too. Put the cocoa in a small bowl and pour over the coffee and hot water, whisking to form a smooth liquid. Set aside.

2. Put the butter and chocolate into a medium heatproof bowl set over a pan of gently simmering water, making sure the base of the bowl doesn't touch the water. Heat until fully melted, stirring frequently. Remove from the heat and set aside.

3. Whisk the sugar and eggs together until pale and thickened. Pour in the chocolate mixture and whisk to combine. Sift the flour and baking powder over the chocolate mixture and fold together until fully combined. Stir in the cocoa mixture. Divide the mixture equally between the two prepared tins and bake for 30 minutes or until the cakes spring back when lightly touched and a skewer inserted into the centre comes out clean. Allow the cakes to cool in the tins for 10 minutes before turning out onto a wire rack to cool completely.

4. To make the buttercream, melt the chocolate in a heatproof bowl set over a pan of gently simmering water, making sure the base of the bowl doesn't touch the water. Remove from the heat and allow to cool. Put the butter into a large bowl and, using an electric mixer, beat until light and creamy, about 3 minutes. Slowly pour in the cream, mixing until fully combined.

5. Add the icing sugar, a little at a time. Once fully combined, add the salt and beat on high speed until the buttercream is light and fluffy. Pour in the cooled chocolate and mix until fully combined.

6. To assemble the cake, put the first cake layer onto a cardboard cake round or serving plate. If the cake is domed, use a serrated knife to level it. Top with a layer of the buttercream. Trim the second layer in the same way, if necessary, then place on top of the first. Cover the cake with the remaining buttercream. Put the cake in the fridge for 20–30 minutes before coating it with the sugarpaste.

7. To decorate the cake, first create the white base layer. Take the white sugarpaste and knead it until pliable. The colder the sugarpaste the longer it will need to be worked with to soften it. Lightly dust the work surface with a little icing sugar and then roll out the sugarpaste into a circle large enough to cover the cake. The easiest way to do this is to take a piece of string and use it as a guide. Drape it over the cake and grip it where it meets the table. Lift the string from the cake and use this as a measure for your sugarpaste. Using the flats of your hands and arms, gently drape the sugarpaste over the cake, and use your hands to smooth the top, applying a gentle pressure. Carefully work your way around the cake, gently smoothing the sugarpaste onto the sides, and trim off the excess.

8. To decorate the cake as I have done, take the coloured sugarpaste and roll it out into a 28cm circle. Use a knife to cut out drip shapes all around the circle, making sure to leave the central 20cm free of cuts. Lightly brush the cake with a little water and then drape the sugarpaste over the cake. The water will act as a glue. Alternatively, you can decorate the cake in any way you want.

28

Red Velvet Cheesecake

SERVES 8

For the base	For the chocolate cheesecake
200g **Oreo cookies** with the filling scraped off (about 2 packets)	100g **dark chocolate** (about 70% cocoa solids), finely chopped
about 80g **unsalted butter**, melted	250g **full-fat cream cheese**
pinch of **sea salt**	5 tbsp **caster sugar**
	150ml **double cream**
	1–2 tsp **red gel food colouring**

For the topping
250ml **double cream**

Originally from the US, red velvet is definitely a firm favourite. Not so long ago, people in the UK would probably have looked at you a little confused if you had offered them a red velvet cupcake, but now you can even buy them in supermarkets and it's one of the most popular flavours at bakeries across the country. I have taken the flavours and transferred it to a no-bake cheesecake.

1. Put the cookies in a medium bowl and, using the end of a rolling pin, crush them until fine. Add the butter and sea salt and mix well. Squeeze some of the mixture in your hand; it should stick together. If not, add a little extra butter. Tip the mixture into a 23cm pie plate and press firmly over the base and sides. Put the pie plate in the fridge until needed.

2. To make the cheesecake, melt the chocolate in a heatproof bowl set over a pan of gently simmering water, making sure the base of the bowl doesn't touch the water. Remove from the heat and allow to cool.

3. Beat the cream cheese and sugar together in a medium bowl until smooth and creamy. In a medium bowl whisk together the cream and food colouring until the cream holds soft peaks. Pour in the melted chocolate and gently mix together. Add the cream mixture to the cream cheese mixture and fold together until evenly combined. Pour the mixture onto the prepared biscuit base and smooth out.

4. Chill for 2 hours or until set. Before serving, put the double cream for the topping in a medium bowl and whisk until it holds soft peaks. Spread the cream over the top of the cheesecake.

Victoria Sandwich

SERVES 10

225g **self-raising flour**
2 tsp **baking powder**
225g **unsalted butter** at room
  temperature
225g **caster sugar**
4 large **eggs**, lightly beaten
1–2 tbsp **milk**, if needed
120g **raspberry jam**
150ml **double cream**, whipped
  to soft peaks
icing or **caster sugar**, for dusting

I was once asked what cake I would choose if I could eat only one type for the rest of my life, and unexpectedly I chose this: the humble Victoria Sandwich. Although it is basic and very easy to make, there is something delicious about its simplicity. I don't know anyone who dislikes it – it really seems to have universal appeal.

1. Preheat the oven to 180°C (160°C fan oven) mark 4, then lightly grease and line two 20cm cake tins with baking parchment, greasing the parchment too.

2. In a medium bowl, whisk the flour and baking powder together to combine, then set aside.

3. Put the butter and sugar into a large bowl and, using an electric mixer, beat until light and fluffy, about 5 minutes. Add the eggs, a little at a time, beating until fully combined.

4. With the mixer on low, add the flour mixture in three additions until just combined. The cake batter should be a 'dropping consistency', which means that if you take a spoonful of batter out of the bowl it should be light enough to fall easily from the spoon. If the batter is sticking to the spoon for too long, mix in 1–2 tbsp milk to soften the batter.

5. Divide the cake batter evenly between the two prepared cake tins and gently level out. Bake for 25 minutes or until golden brown and coming away from the edge of the tin; a cocktail stick inserted into the centre of a cake should come out clean. Allow to cool in the tin for 10 minutes before turning out onto a wire rack to cool completely.

6. To assemble the cake, spread one layer of cake with the jam and top with the whipped cream. Sandwich together with the second layer of cake, and sprinkle with a little icing or caster sugar.

Meringues

MAKES 6

150g **egg whites** (about 4 large eggs)
300g **caster sugar**

For rose and pistachio meringues
1 tbsp **rose syrup**
40g **pistachio nuts,** finely chopped

For chocolate meringues
1 tbsp **cocoa powder**

For fruit meringues
10g **freeze-dried fruit,** crushed to a fine powder

I love walking past bakeries that have piles of large meringues in the window. They look like soft pillowy clouds and they often have vibrant colours that just look so pretty. Making meringues is actually really easy and recreating the shop-bought versions is very simple. You can make traditional white ones or flavour them.

1. Preheat the oven to 130°C (110°C fan oven) mark ½ and line a baking sheet with baking parchment.

2. Put the egg whites and sugar into a large, grease-free heatproof bowl set over a pan of gently simmering water, making sure the base of the bowl doesn't touch the water. Using an electric mixer, whisk constantly until the sugar has dissolved and the egg mixture is just warm to the touch. The easiest way to test this is to dip your thumb and forefinger into the mixture and rub them together; if you can feel sugar, continue whisking a little longer. Remove from the heat and whisk the meringue until stiff and glossy.

3. If you want to make flavoured meringues, fold in any of the suggested options, leaving a little of the flavouring to sprinkle on top of the meringues before baking.

4. For plain or flavoured meringues, using a large metal spoon, place 6 large dollops of the meringue onto the prepared baking sheet a few centimetres apart from each other. Sprinkle over a little of the flavourings, if using. Bake for 1½ hours, then turn off the heat and allow the meringues to cool completely in the oven.

33

Mix & Match Cupcakes

What better to way to entertain a party full of kids than a cupcake-decorating session? Have everything ready to go and let the kids go wild and decorate the cakes as they fancy.

MAKES 12

<u>Vanilla cupcakes</u>
175g **plain flour**
2¼ tsp **baking powder**
¼ tsp **salt**
115g **unsalted butter**, at room temperature
200g **caster sugar**
2 large **eggs**, lightly beaten
1 tsp **vanilla extract**
150ml **buttermilk**

MAKES 12

<u>Chocolate cupcakes</u>
40g **cocoa powder**
140ml boiling **water**
70ml **buttermilk**
40ml **vegetable oil**
170g **soft light brown sugar**
1 tsp **vanilla extract**
1 large **egg**
1 large **egg yolk**

140g **plain flour**
1 tsp **bicarbonate of soda**
¼ tsp **salt**

1. Preheat the oven to 180°C (160°C fan oven) mark 4 and line a standard 12-cup muffin pan with paper cases. In a medium bowl whisk the flour, baking powder and salt together to combine, then set aside.

2. Put the butter and sugar into a large bowl and, using an electric mixer, beat until light and fluffy, about 5 minutes. Add the eggs and vanilla extract a little at a time, beating until fully combined.

3. Add the flour mixture in three additions, alternating with the buttermilk, starting and finishing with the flour mixture. Divide the batter among the prepared muffin cups, filling each case about half-full. Bake for 22–25 minutes or until a cocktail stick inserted into the centre of a cake comes out clean.

1. Preheat the oven to 180°C (160°C fan oven) mark 4 and line a standard 12-cup muffin pan with paper cases.

2. Put the cocoa powder and boiling water into a large bowl and mix until the cocoa is fully dissolved.

3. Add the buttermilk, oil, light brown sugar and vanilla extract, and mix to combine.

4. Mix in the egg and egg yolk, then add the flour, bicarbonate of soda and salt, and mix until just combined.

5. Divide the batter between the muffin cups filling each case about half-full. Bake for 15–18 minutes or until a cocktail stick inserted into the centre of a cake comes out clean.

34

FOR 12 CUPCAKES

Italian meringue buttercream
150g **caster sugar**
3 large **egg whites** .
270g **unsalted butter**, at room
temperature

1. To make the buttercream, put 95ml water and the sugar into a pan over medium heat. Bring to the boil and have a sugar thermometer ready.

2. Meanwhile, put the egg whites into a clean, grease-free bowl (this is best done using a freestanding electric mixer). Start whisking the whites on high speed when the syrup in the pan reaches about 115°C on the sugar thermometer. Cook until the syrup registers 121°C. With the mixer still running, pour the syrup in a slow stream down the side of the bowl containing the whites, avoiding the beaters. Continue whisking on high speed until the meringue is at room temperature.

3. With the mixer on medium–high speed add the butter, a few pieces at a time, beating until fully combined. When adding the butter it can sometimes look curdled; if this happens don't worry, just keep mixing and eventually it will smooth out again forming a light buttercream.

4. Flavourings: once the buttercream is made you could add 100g dark chocolate (about 70% cocoa solids), melted and cooled, or 125g raspberry jam or lemon curd, if you like.

FOR 12 CUPCAKES

Classic vanilla buttercream
250g **unsalted butter**, at room
temperature
2 tsp **vanilla bean paste**
100ml **double cream**
500g **icing sugar**, sifted
a pinch of **salt**

FOR 12 CUPCAKES

Whipped ganache frosting
200g **dark chocolate** (about 70%
cocoa solids), finely chopped
200ml **double cream**

1. Beat the butter and vanilla paste using an electric mixer until light and creamy. With the mixer on medium speed, slowly incorporate the double cream. Once light and smooth, slowly incorporate the icing sugar and salt, and then beat on high speed until light and fluffy.

2. Flavourings: I prefer this classic buttercream as it is, but you could mix in 125g lemon curd after adding the icing sugar, if you like, or flavour it with melted chocolate or raspberry jam as for the Italian meringue buttercream.

1. Put the chocolate in a large heatproof bowl and set aside. Put the cream in a small pan over medium heat and bring just to the boil. Pour over the chocolate and allow to stand for 2 minutes before gently stirring together to form a silky smooth ganache. Cool in the fridge for a few minutes until it just begins to thicken. It should be shiny and pourable, looking a little like thick custard. Whisk in short bursts until the mixture is just holding its shape.

2. This frosting isn't easy to pipe because it will easily melt when held in a piping bag, so I prefer to use an offset spatula to apply it.

Chocolate & Amaretto Baked Alaska

SERVES 6

butter, for greasing	**For the amaretto Swiss meringue**
4 large **eggs**	80g **egg whites** (about
100g **caster sugar**	2 large eggs)
60g **plain flour**	190g **caster sugar**
40g **cocoa powder**	¼ tsp **cream of tartar**
500ml tub of **chocolate ice cream**, softened	2 tbsp **amaretto**

For the amaretto syrup
50g **caster sugar**
2–3 tbsp **amaretto**

The combination of chocolate and amaretto is one of my favourites, and used in a baked Alaska it turns an old-fashioned dessert into something completely different. Although there are a few more steps of preparation than is usual for a basic baked Alaska, this version is so much more rewarding both in looks and, of course, in taste.

1. Preheat the oven to 180°C (160°C fan oven) mark 4, then grease a 27 × 39cm high-sided baking tray and line with baking parchment, greasing the parchment too. Put the eggs and sugar into a heatproof bowl set over a pan of gently simmering water, making sure the bowl doesn't touch the water. Whisk constantly until the sugar has dissolved and the mixture is just warm to the touch.

2. Remove the bowl from the pan and, using an electric mixer, whisk for 5 minutes on high speed, then reduce the speed to medium and whisk for a further 3 minutes. By this stage the mixture should have tripled in volume, and when the whisk is lifted from the bowl it should form a slowly dissolving ribbon.

3. Sift in the flour and cocoa powder, and gently fold together, making sure all the dry ingredients are combined but trying to keep as much volume as possible. Pour the batter into the prepared tin and very gently level it out. Bake for 15 minutes or until the cake is risen and a skewer inserted into the centre of the cake comes out clean. Allow to cool in the tin for 10 minutes before turning out onto a wire rack to cool completely.

4. To make the syrup, put 50ml water and the sugar in a small pan and bring to a boil, then simmer for about 2 minutes or until the sugar is fully dissolved. Remove from the heat and add the amaretto to taste. Take a 1 litre (16cm wide) pudding bowl and line with a piece of clingfilm, leaving a large overhang.

5. Cut out two discs of cake, one to fit the top and one to fit the base of the bowl, and use the remaining cake to cut out a strip to line the sides of the bowl. Line the bowl with the base and side sponge pieces and brush liberally with the syrup.

6. Fill with the ice cream and put the larger sponge disc on top, then press firmly to seal. Fold over the clingfilm and freeze for about 1 hour or until the ice cream is firm.

7. To assemble the dessert, put the egg whites, sugar and cream of tartar for the amaretto Swiss meringue into a grease-free heatproof bowl set over a pan of gently simmering water. Using an electric mixer, whisk constantly until the sugar has dissolved. Remove the bowl from the heat and whisk until the meringue forms stiff, glossy peaks. Add the amaretto and whisk to combine.

8. Remove the ice cream-filled cake from the freezer and unwrap, then turn out onto a serving plate. Pour the meringue onto the sponge and spread evenly to cover completely. Use a blowtorch to brown the meringue, or brown it in the oven preheated to 230°C (210°C fan oven) mark 8 for 3–4 minutes.

TIP

If you want to make this a spectacular finish to a meal, you can take a small pan with 40ml amaretto and gently warm it over low heat. Once ready to serve, light the amaretto and pour it over the Baked Alaska.

36

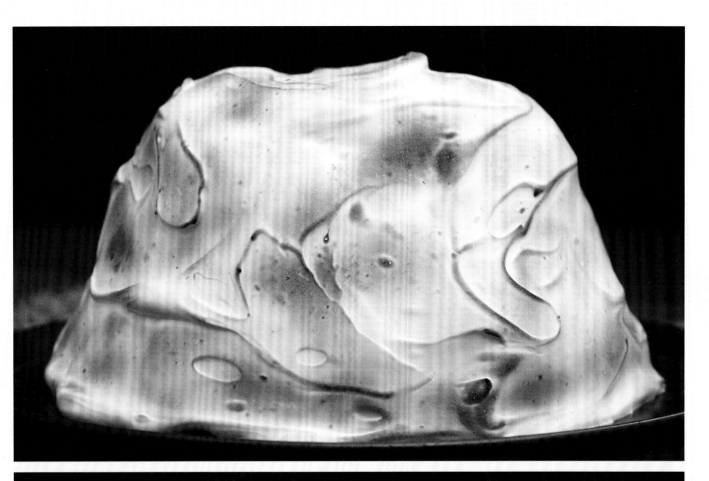

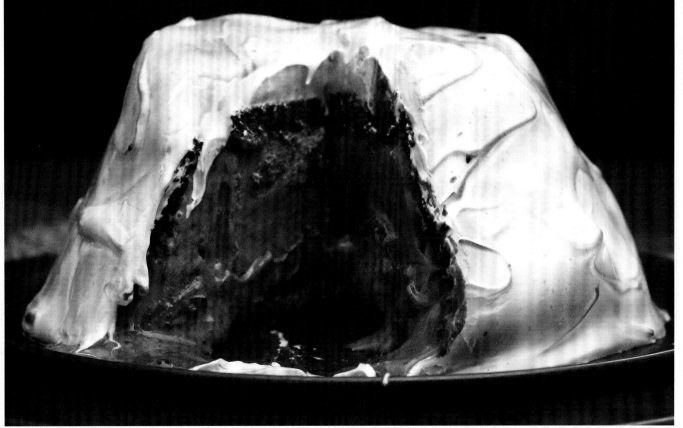

Fresh Blueberry Marshmallows

MAKES ABOUT 45

oil spray, for greasing
425g **caster sugar**
1 tbsp **liquid glucose.**
8 sheets of **gelatine**
2 large **egg whites**
150g **blueberries**

For the coating
50g **icing sugar**
50g **cornflour**

You may think that it is difficult to make marshmallows, but that couldn't be further from the truth. If you can make a meringue, you can make marshmallows. These ones are pillowy soft and they melt in your mouth. To counteract the sweetness, I have added some fresh blueberries, which pop in your mouth as you eat the marshmallows – delicious!

1. Lightly grease a 23 × 33cm high-sided baking tray or brownie pan, then line with a piece of clingfilm and lightly grease the clingfilm. To make the coating, mix the icing sugar and cornflour together and dust the clingfilm with a thin layer of this mixture, reserving the remainder.

2. Put the sugar, glucose and 125ml water into a medium pan over medium heat. Bring to the boil and have a sugar thermometer ready.

3. Meanwhile, put the gelatine into a medium bowl and cover with 150ml cold water.

4. Also, put the egg whites into a clean, grease-free bowl (this is best done using a freestanding electric mixer). Start whisking the whites on high speed to form soft peaks when the syrup in the pan reaches about 115°C on the sugar thermometer. Cook until the syrup registers 118°C. With the mixer still running, pour the syrup in a slow stream down the side of the bowl containing the whites, avoiding the beaters.

5. Put the softened gelatine and the water into the now empty syrup pan over low heat, then stir until the gelatine is fully melted. Pour this mixture into the meringue mixture and continue whisking until the mixture is cool.

6. Pour half this marshmallow mixture into the prepared tray and, using an oiled spatula, spread into an even layer. Sprinkle over the blueberries and then top with the remaining marshmallow. Sprinkle the top of the marshmallow with a thin layer of the coating and then allow to set at room temperature for a few hours.

7. Once fully set, tip the marshmallow out onto a sheet of baking parchment and cut into squares using either a pizza wheel or scissors. Roll the marshmallows in the remaining coating and then shake off the excess.

8. Store in a sealed container; the marshmallows will keep for a few days (but without the blueberries they will keep for at least a week).

Jelly and Custard Cups

MAKES 6

650g mixed **summer fruits**
  (such as **strawberries**,
  raspberries, **blackberries**,
  blackcurrants and
  redcurrants)
4 tbsp **caster sugar**
about 80ml **water or prosecco**
4 leaves of **gelatine**
icing sugar, for dusting

For the custard
1 **vanilla pod**
400ml **whole milk**
35g **caster sugar**
2 tsp **cornflour**
4 large **egg yolks**

These jellies are firmly rooted in my childhood, like many of my ideas. I remember eating a lot of jelly as a child, at home, at school and at parties when I was little. Although there is nothing wrong with a simple and classic jelly, these look a little more refined, and if you make them with prosecco (not for the kids, of course), they have a very adult twist.

1. Put 500g mixed summer fruits, the sugar and 80ml water or prosecco into a large pan over medium heat. Cook gently, stirring occasionally, until the fruit has softened and released a lot of its juice. Strain the fruit through a sieve into a measuring jug, setting the softened fruit aside (it isn't needed for the recipe but would be lovely served with some ice cream). You will need 400ml of liquid, so top up as required with water or prosecco.

2. Put the gelatine into a small pan and pour over a little of the fruit juice, just enough to cover the gelatine. Allow this mixture to soften for 10 minutes, then place over low heat and stir until the gelatine is fully dissolved. Pour this mixture back into the remaining fruit juice and stir to combine. Divide the jelly mixture among six small glasses and chill for 4–6 hours until fully set.

3. To make the custard, scrape the seeds from the vanilla pod, then put the pod and seeds into a medium pan with the milk, and bring to the boil then a simmer over medium heat.

4. Whisk the sugar and cornflour together in a medium heatproof bowl. Add the egg yolks and whisk together until pale and thickened.

5. Remove the vanilla pod from the milk, and then pour half the hot milk over the eggs, whisking constantly. Pour back into the pan and cook over medium heat, whisking constantly until it thickens. Pour into a jug and leave to cool slightly, then divide among the six glasses. Chill until ready to serve. To serve, top each glass with a little of the remaining fresh fruit and a light dusting of icing sugar.

MY SISTER AND BROTHER, NICOLA AND NEIL

39

TIP

If you prefer a more classic profiterole with cream instead of the praline filling, whip 600ml double cream with 1 tsp vanilla bean paste and 2 tbsp icing sugar until it just forms stiff peaks, and use this instead.

Praline Profiterole Tower

85g **plain flour**	6 large **egg yolks**
60g **unsalted butter**	50g **caster sugar**
¼ tsp **caster sugar**	4 tbsp **plain flour**
¼ tsp **salt**	2 tsp **vanilla extract**
2–3 large **eggs**	
	For the chocolate sauce
For the hazelnut praline	75g **dark chocolate** (about
100g skinned **hazelnuts**	70% cocoa solids), finely
100g **caster sugar**	chopped
	10g **unsalted butter**
For the pastry cream	1 tbsp **clear honey**
450ml **whole milk**	150ml **double cream**

I know profiteroles are a bit retro, but I love them. There is nothing wrong with choux pastry, cream and chocolate – it's a classic for a reason. For a more modern version, I fill the buns with pastry cream mixed with hazelnut praline; they are richer than the classic so the portion sizes should be smaller. To sterilise the jars for the praline paste, wash in very hot water then place into a warm oven until ready to use.

1. To make the hazelnut praline, preheat the oven to 200°C (180°C fan oven) mark 6. Put the hazelnuts on a baking sheet lined with baking parchment and put into the hot oven for 5 minutes or until fragrant. Remove from the oven and allow to cool. Put the sugar into a medium pan over medium heat and allow to dissolve and cook until dark golden brown in colour, stopping before it starts to smoke.

2. Immediately pour the caramel carefully over the hazelnuts, then leave to cool. Break into pieces and put into the bowl of a food processor. Pulse to break the pieces into smaller chunks, then process until you have a smooth paste, this will take a few minutes. Put the praline paste into a sterilised jar. (This can be prepared days ahead, as it keeps very well.)

3. To make the pastry cream, put the milk into a large pan over medium heat and bring to the boil. Meanwhile, in a medium bowl, whisk the egg yolks, sugar, flour and vanilla extract until pale and smooth. Pour in half of the hot milk and whisk to combine. Pour the egg mixture back into the pan and put back on the heat. Bring to the boil, whisking constantly, until thickened. Pour the pastry cream into a bowl and press a piece of clingfilm onto the surface to stop a skin forming. Cool and chill.

4. For the choux buns line two baking sheets with baking parchment. Sift the flour onto a sheet of greaseproof paper. Put the butter, sugar, salt and 140ml water into a medium pan over medium–high heat and bring to a rolling boil. Take off the heat and tip in the flour. Using a wooden spoon, beat to combine. Put back on the heat and beat the dough for a few minutes or until the dough comes away from the sides of the pan.

5. Tip the dough into a medium bowl and beat vigorously until no longer steaming. Beat in the eggs, one at a time – you may not need them all; check the consistency of the dough after each addition. It should be smooth and shiny and will fall from the wooden spoon forming a V-shaped ribbon. If it looks almost right after 2 eggs, just add a little of the third and test again. Put the dough into a piping bag fitted with a plain piping tip and pipe into rounds on the prepared baking sheet about 2.5cm in diameter. Using a finger dipped in water, gently tap any peaks down.

6. Bake for 20–25 minutes or until risen and golden brown. Remove the tray from the oven and, using a sharp knife, make a hole in the base of each choux bun. Turn the oven off and put the choux buns back into the oven, base up, for 10 minutes; this will help keep the buns crisp.

7. To fill the buns, take the pastry cream out of the fridge and beat in the praline paste. Put the praline cream into a piping bag fitted with a small plain piping tip and fill each bun with cream.

8. To make the chocolate sauce, put the chocolate, butter, honey and cream into a small pan and cook over medium heat, stirring occasionally, until the chocolate melts and the sauce is smooth and fully combined. Pour into a jug and allow to cool slightly. The longer you leave the sauce the thicker it will become. To thin it out, gently heat it up until the desired consistency. To serve the profiteroles, take a large plate and pile the choux buns in the middle. Drizzle over the warm chocolate sauce, and then dig in!

Zuccotto Summer Pudding

Summer pudding is a stalwart of British cooking. Normally made with stale bread it is a classic that is very easy to put together. My version crosses the British classic with an Italian classic, zuccotto, which is similar in presentation except that it is a cake filled with a cream or ice cream mixture. My dessert combines the best of both worlds.

SERVES 8–10

25g **unsalted butter**, melted and cooled, plus extra butter for greasing	**For the fruit filling** 600g **summer fruits** (such as strawberries, raspberries, blueberries, redcurrants, blackberries and cherries)
4 large **eggs** 100g **caster sugar** 100g **plain flour** **cream**, to serve (optional)	125g **caster sugar** 2 tbsp **crème de cassis**
	For the cream filling 240ml **double cream** 1 tbsp **icing sugar** 1 tsp **vanilla bean paste**

1. Preheat the oven to 180°C (160°C fan oven) mark 4, then line a 27 × 39cm high-sided baking tray with baking parchment, greasing the parchment too. Put the eggs and sugar into a heatproof bowl set over a pan of gently simmering water, making sure the base of the bowl doesn't touch the water. Whisk constantly until the sugar has dissolved and the mixture is just warm to the touch.

2. Remove from the heat and, using an electric mixer, whisk for 5 minutes on high speed, then reduce the speed to medium and whisk for a further 3 minutes. By this stage the mixture should have tripled in volume, and when the whisk is lifted from the bowl it should form a slowly dissolving ribbon.

3. Sift in the flour and gently fold together making sure all the ingredients are combined but trying to keep as much volume as possible. Take a large spoonful of the batter and add to the melted butter, then mix together (this will lighten the butter and help to incorporate it into the batter). Gently fold this into the batter.

4. Pour the batter into the prepared tin and very gently level out. Bake for 15 minutes or until the cake is risen; a skewer inserted into the centre of the cake should come out clean. Allow to cool in the tin for 10 minutes before turning out onto a wire rack to cool completely.

5. To make the filling, put all the ingredients into a medium pan and cook over medium heat until the fruit has softened slightly and there is a vibrant syrup in the base of the pan. Drain the fruit and set aside, reserving the syrup.

6. To make the cream filling, whisk all the ingredients together until the cream holds stiff peaks. To assemble the pudding, line a 1 litre bowl with clingfilm, making sure there is an overhang to help remove the pudding later. Cut out two discs of cake, one to fit the base of the bowl and one to fit the top. Cut the remaining cake into thin strips.

7. Dip all the cake into the reserved syrup and use all but the top piece to line the prepared bowl. Spread the cream filling across the base and up the sides of the bowl, covering all the cake. Tip the fruit into the bowl and seal with the larger disc of cake. Press a piece of clingfilm to the top of the pudding and put a small plate on top. Put a weight, such as a tin of beans, onto the plate to weight it down. This helps to seal the pudding so that it holds its shape. Chill for 4–5 hours before serving.

8. Remove the weight and plate, and turn the bowl over onto a serving plate. Use the overhang of clingfilm to tease the pudding from the bowl. Serve on its own or with a little extra cream.

romance

Love Heart Cookies

MAKES ABOUT 30	For the decoration
425g **plain flour**, plus extra for dusting	700g **white sugarpaste**
½ tsp **salt**	**red gel food colouring**
200g **caster sugar**	225g **royal icing sugar**
225g **unsalted butter**, diced and chilled	**icing sugar**, for dusting
1 large **egg**	
1 large **egg yolk**	
1 tsp **vanilla bean paste**	

Love heart sweets might just taste of sugar, but they are undeniably cute. I remember passing them around at primary school, and it was very important that you chose your message carefully. Why not bake these cookies based on the childhood sweets and use them as a fun and personal favour for a wedding? You can tailor the message to whatever you like, be it the wedding couple's names or simply words of love.

1. Line two baking sheets with baking parchment. Put the flour, salt and sugar in the bowl of a food processor and pulse to combine. Add the butter and pulse until the mixture resembles coarse breadcrumbs. (Alternatively, rub the butter into the flour mixture by hand or using a pastry cutter, to resemble coarse breadcrumbs.) Add the egg, yolk and vanilla paste and pulse (or stir) until the mixture just comes together. Tip onto a lightly floured work surface and gently knead together until uniform. Divide the dough in half and wrap in clingfilm, then chill for about 1 hour.

2. Working with one half of the dough at a time, roll out to a thickness of 5mm. Cut out rounds using a 9cm cookie cutter. Re-roll the scraps to cut out more biscuits. Lift the cookies off the surface with a spatula and put them onto the prepared baking sheets, then chill for 15–20 minutes. Preheat the oven to 180°C (160°C fan oven) mark 4.

3. Bake for 13–15 minutes or until the edges turn golden. Allow to cool on the baking sheets for 10 minutes before transferring to a wire rack to cool completely.

4. To decorate, take the sugarpaste and knead it until pliable. Knead a few drops of red food colouring into the sugarpaste to make it light pink. Wrap the sugarpaste in clingfilm while you make the royal icing. Sift the royal icing sugar into a medium bowl and add 30ml water. Beat with a wooden spoon until combined. Using a cocktail stick, add a little colouring to make the icing red. The royal icing should be barely pourable, so if it's too thin, add a little extra icing sugar; if it's too thick, add a little more water.

5. Roll out the sugarpaste on a work surface dusted with a little icing sugar until it is about 2mm thick. Cut out 9cm rounds with the cookie cutter. Put the royal icing in a piping bag fitted with a thin round (about 2mm) piping tip and pipe a swirl of icing onto each cookie. Put the rounds of sugarpaste onto the cookies. Use the remaining royal icing to pipe the decoration: first pipe a circle around the outside edge of the cookie, and then pipe a heart in the centre. To replicate the look of the love heart sweets, you can then pipe words and phrases inside the heart.

Flourless Chocolate & Blackberry Cake

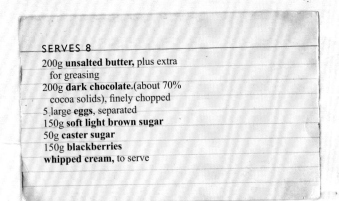

SERVES 8

200g **unsalted butter,** plus extra
for greasing
200g **dark chocolate.**(about 70%
cocoa solids), finely chopped
5 large **eggs,** separated
150g **soft light brown sugar**
50g **caster sugar**
150g **blackberries**
whipped cream, to serve

Everyone knows that chocolate is the ultimate romantic food, and this cake is pure romance. A gooey warm flourless cake studded with little bursts of blackberry – it's the perfect dish to make for a date or Valentine's dinner. It will most definitely impress.

1. Preheat the oven to 180°C (160°C fan oven) mark 4, then line the base of a 23cm springform cake tin with baking parchment, greasing the parchment too. Set a heatproof bowl over a pan of lightly simmering water, making sure the base of the bowl doesn't touch the water. Add the chocolate and butter to the bowl and allow to melt, stirring occasionally.

2. In a medium bowl, whisk the egg yolks and light brown sugar together until thickened and pale. Put the egg whites into a clean, grease-free bowl and whisk until they form firm peaks, then slowly pour in the caster sugar and whisk until the meringue is stiff and glossy.

3. Whisk the chocolate mixture into the egg yolk mixture, then stir in a third of the meringue to lighten the batter. Gently fold in the remaining meringue, trying to knock out as little air as possible.

4. Pour the batter into the prepared tin and gently level out. Sprinkle over the blackberries and bake for 35–40 minutes or until the cake is risen and has thin cracks on top. Allow the cake to cool in the tin for 10 minutes before removing the springform collar and cooling on a wire rack.

5. When warm, this cake is very light and melts on the tongue. If you prefer a slightly firmer texture, allow the cake to cool completely and then pop it into the fridge; served cold it will have a slightly brownie-type texture. Serve with a little whipped cream.

Rose & Raspberry Cheesecake

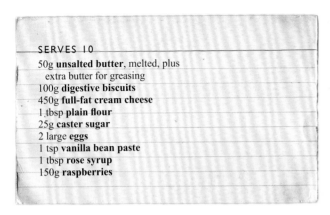

SERVES 10

50g **unsalted butter**, melted, plus
 extra butter for greasing
100g **digestive biscuits**
450g **full-fat cream cheese**
1 tbsp **plain flour**
25g **caster sugar**
2 large **eggs**
1 tsp **vanilla bean paste**
1 tbsp **rose syrup**
150g **raspberries**

A rose for a romantic occasion is traditional and a classic, so why mess with a classic? Adding the rose syrup and raspberry to this cheesecake cuts the richness and adds a delicate floral note, it's definitely not soapy or overpowering.

1. Preheat the oven to 180°C (160°C fan oven) mark 4, then grease and line a 20cm springform cake tin with baking parchment. Put the digestive biscuits into a medium bowl and, using the base of a rolling pin, crush them into fine crumbs. Add the melted butter and stir to coat evenly.

2. Firmly press the mixture into the base of the prepared tin. Bake for 10 minutes, or until the edges turn golden, then remove from the oven and allow to cool while you make the filling. Reduce the oven to 150°C (130°C fan oven) mark 2.

3. Put the cream cheese and flour into a large bowl and, using an electric mixer, beat until smooth. Add the sugar and beat until just combined – the less you beat a baked cheesecake mixture the better; if you over-beat, the cake will have a higher chance of developing cracks.

4. Lightly beat the eggs and vanilla paste together, and slowly incorporate this mixture into the cream cheese mixture, beating until just fully combined. Pour about a quarter of the mixture into another bowl and stir in the rose syrup.

5. Add the raspberries to the larger portion of mixture and pour onto the prepared base, then gently smooth out. Add the rose-flavoured mixture on top and, using a knife, swirl gently into the vanilla mixture. Bake for 1 hour or until the edges are set but the centre is still wobbly. Cool and chill overnight before serving. This firms up the cheesecake and gives it a delicious silky-smooth texture.

49

Concorde

SERVES 10

6 large **egg whites**
60g **caster sugar**
300g **icing sugar**
30g **cocoa powder**
icing sugar or **cocoa powder**,
  for dusting

For the simple chocolate mousse
185g **dark chocolate** (about 70%
  cocoa solids), finely chopped
about 500ml **double cream**

This cake is beautiful and looks so much more complicated to make than it actually is. If you have made meringues before, you will be fine – but if you haven't, don't worry, because it really is very simple. This is my version of a cake created by the famous Parisian chef Gaston Lenôtre in 1969 to celebrate the inaugural flight of Concorde.

1. Preheat the oven to 110°C (90°C fan oven) mark ¼ and line three baking sheets with baking parchment. Using a 20cm cake tin as a template, draw a circle on each piece of parchment, then turn it over so that the drawing is underneath.

2. Put the egg whites into a clean, grease-free bowl and, using an electric mixer, whisk until they form stiff peaks. Slowly pour in the caster sugar and whisk until the meringue is stiff and glossy. Sift the icing sugar and cocoa powder over the meringue and gently fold together, being as gentle as possible.

3. Spoon the meringue into a piping bag fitted with a 1cm wide plain piping tip and pipe three discs on the baking parchment using the drawn templates, piping in a spiral starting at the centre and working outwards. Using the remaining meringue, pipe long strips onto the prepared trays alongside the discs. Bake for about 1 hour 40 minutes or until firm and crisp. Turn off the oven and allow the meringues to cool in the oven for 2 hours.

4. To make the mousse, melt the chocolate in a large heatproof bowl set over a pan of gently simmering water, making sure the base of the bowl doesn't touch the water. Remove from the heat and leave to cool. Whisk the cream to soft peaks then pour it into the bowl with the chocolate and whisk to combine. The resulting mousse should be fairly thick and be able to hold its shape, but not so thick it can't be spread easily. If it is too thick and looks overwhipped, pour in a little extra cream or milk and stir to loosen the mousse.

5. To assemble the cake, use a little of the mousse to stick the first meringue disc to a cardboard cake board or serving plate. Spread about a third of the mousse over the meringue and then add another meringue and repeat the process. Top with the final meringue and then coat the top and sides of the cake with the remaining third of the mousse.

6. To finish the decoration, use a serrated knife to gently cut the meringue strips into pieces. Lightly press these all over the cake and lightly dust with either icing sugar or cocoa powder. You can either serve the cake now or you can freeze it for a few hours; this will soften the meringue slightly. If you do freeze the cake, thaw it in the fridge for a few hours before serving.

TIP

Use a gentle sawing motion when cutting the meringue, as it is very fragile and breaks easily.

Traditional Wedding Cake

SERVES 125

For the large (30.5cm) tier

450g **sultanas**	450g **unsalted butter** at room temperature, plus extra for greasing
450g **currants**	450g **plain flour**
450g **raisins**	230g **ground almonds**
225g **mixed candied peel**	1 tsp **salt**
225g **glacé cherries**, roughly chopped	2 tsp **ground cinnamon**
zest of 2 **oranges**	2 tsp **mixed spice**
zest of 2 **lemons**	450g **caster sugar**
125ml **brandy**	10 large **eggs**

For the medium (23cm) tier

225g **sultanas**	225g **unsalted butter** at room temperature, plus extra for greasing
225g **currants**	225g **plain flour**
225g **raisins**	115g **ground almonds**
115g **mixed candied peel**	½ tsp **salt**
115g **glacé cherries**, roughly chopped	1½ tsp **ground cinnamon**
zest of 1 **orange**	1½ tsp **mixed spice**
zest of 1 **lemon**	225g **caster sugar**
60ml **brandy**	5 large **eggs**

For the small (15cm) tier

115g **sultanas**	115g **unsalted butter** at room temperature, plus extra for greasing
115g **currants**	115g **plain flour**
115g **raisins**	55g **ground almonds**
55g **mixed candied peel**	¼ tsp **salt**
55g **glacé cherries**, roughly chopped	1 tsp **ground cinnamon**
zest of ½ **orange**	1 tsp **mixed spice**
zest of ½ **lemon**	115g **caster sugar**
30ml **brandy**	2½ large **eggs**

For the decoration

340g jar **apricot jam**, sieved
icing sugar, for dusting
3.5kg **marzipan**
3,5kg **white sugarpaste**
1kg **pale-brown sugarpaste**
1kg **teal blue sugarpaste**

Materials

30.5cm, 23cm and 15cm cardboard cake rounds
wooden or plastic dowelling rods
35.5cm cardboard cake drum (optional)
chocolate-brown ribbon

This wedding cake is an absolute classic. It is based on my Nanna's recipe, and my family believes it may have even been the recipe that was used for her own wedding during the Second World War. Because all the ingredients were rationed at the time, her friends and neighbours pooled their ration coupons so that they were able to get enough ingredients together to make the cake for her special day. The cakes take a long time to bake, but fruit cake keeps very well, so you can spread the work over a number of days, or even weeks. If preparing the cakes ahead, wrap them well in clingfilm and store until ready to decorate.

1. The night before you want to make the large cake, put the fruits, zests and brandy into a large bowl and mix together. Cover with clingfilm and leave to soak overnight.

2. Next day, preheat the oven to 160°C (140°C fan oven) mark 2½, then grease and triple-line a deep 30.5cm round cake tin with baking parchment. In a medium bowl whisk the flour, almonds, salt and spices together to combine, then set aside

3. Put the butter and sugar into a large bowl and, using an electric mixer, beat until light and fluffy, about 5 minutes. Beat in the eggs, a little at a time, beating until fully combined. With the mixer on low, add the flour mixture, a large spoonful at a time, mixing just until combined. Using a large spatula or metal spoon, fold in the fruit.

4. Scrape the batter into the prepared tin and bake for 4 hours or until a cocktail stick inserted into the centre comes out clean. If the cake is browning too quickly, put a tent of foil over the top. Allow the cake to cool completely in the tin before removing.

5. Repeat the process for the other layers, baking the 23cm cake for 3 hours and the 15cm cake for 2 hours.

6. To decorate the cakes you need the tops to have a level surface; if the cakes are domed, use a serrated knife to trim them level. Turn the cakes upside down onto the cake boards so that you have the perfect base as the top: put the medium and small cakes onto their respective cake rounds and the large cake onto the cake drum. Put the apricot jam into a small pan and heat gently to melt. Brush the large cake with a thin layer of the jam, which will act as a glue for the marzipan.

7. Dust the work surface lightly with icing sugar, then roll out 1.75kg of the marzipan until it is large enough to cover the top and sides of the large cake. The easiest way to do this is to take a piece of string and use it as a guide. Drape it over the cake and grip it where it meets the table. Lift the string from the cake and use this as a measure for your marzipan. Using the flats of your hands and arms, gently drape the marzipan onto the cake, smoothing it carefully down the sides of the cake. Use a knife to trim off any excess. Allow the marzipan to dry out for a day before covering in sugarpaste.

8. Take 1.75kg of the white sugarpaste and knead it until pliable. The colder the sugarpaste the longer it will need to be worked with to soften it. Dust a work surface lightly with icing sugar. Roll out the sugarpaste until it is large enough to cover the top and sides of the cake. Brush the marzipan with a little water to create a slightly tacky surface. Using the flats of your hands and arms, gently drape the sugarpaste over the cake, and use your hands to smooth the top, applying a gentle pressure. Carefully work your way around the cake, gently smoothing the sugarpaste onto the sides, and trim off the excess.

9. Repeat this process with the other two cakes using 1kg of sugarpaste and marzipan for the 23cm cake and 500g of both for the 15cm cake.

10. For the decoration, take the chocolate-brown sugarpaste and roll it until 1–2mm thick, then cut out as many strips as possible, in different widths 2–4cm wide. Repeat with the teal blue sugarpaste. You now need to 'glue' these strips to all three cakes. I like to attach them in a random fashion, so that the cake doesn't look symmetrical. For the two largest tiers, cut the strips into lengths that are long enough to go up the sides of the cake and about 5cm towards the centre, but not all the way. For the top tier, the strips need to be long enough to cover the cake, as the top will be visible. To attach the strips, brush them lightly with a little water and press the wet sides to the cakes. Allow these to dry and adhere to the cake before assembling the cake.

11. When ready to assemble, push four dowelling rods into the 30.5cm cake about 5cm in from the outside edge, then mark where they are flush with the sugarpaste. Now remove the dowels and cut them to fit, then push them back inside the cake. Repeat the process with the 23cm cake. These dowels will act as a support so that the cakes won't sink into each other when stacked.

12. Transport the cakes as separate layers. To assemble, put the large cake onto a large cake stand or a cardboard cake drum and centre the medium cake on top followed by the small cake. To finish the decoration, put a strip of ribbon around the base of each cake, using double-sided sticky tape to secure the join. I also like to top the cake with a few flowers, preferably the same ones used in the wedding.

FAMILY WEDDING

Neapolitan Wedding Cake

SERVES 50

For the large (23cm) vanilla cake
butter or oil, for greasing
6 large eggs
150g caster sugar
2 tsp vanilla bean paste
150g plain flour

For the large (23cm) chocolate cake
6 large eggs
150g caster sugar
2 tsp vanilla bean paste
90g plain flour
60g cocoa powder

For the small (15cm) vanilla cake
3 large eggs
75g caster sugar
1 tsp vanilla bean paste
75g plain flour

For the small (15cm) chocolate cake
3 large eggs
75g caster sugar
1 tsp vanilla bean paste
45g plain flour
30g cocoa powder

For the strawberry buttercream
250g caster sugar
5 large egg whites
450g unsalted butter at room temperature
250g seedless strawberry jam

For the simple vanilla syrup
150g caster sugar
2 tsp vanilla extract

For the decoration
600g fresh strawberries

Materials
30.5cm cardboard cake drum or cake stand
3 wooden or plastic dowelling rods
15cm thin cardboard cake round

As a kid I loved the idea of Neapolitan ice cream, but I was always disappointed with the taste. I always left the chocolate section, because so often the flavour just wasn't very nice. The colour and flavours did, however, stay with me, and this modern wedding cake is inspired by that classic of the supermarket freezer aisle. Unlike traditional fruit or sponge wedding cakes, this cake is made with a genoise sponge as its base, and because of this it can actually be easily made in one day because it takes relatively little time to bake.

MY PARENTS' WEDDING DAY

1. To make the large vanilla cake, preheat the oven to 180°C (160°C fan oven) mark 4, then grease and line a deep 23cm cake tin with baking parchment, greasing the parchment too. Put the eggs, sugar and vanilla into a large heatproof bowl set over a pan of gently simmering water, making sure the base of the bowl doesn't touch the water.

2. Whisk the eggs constantly until the sugar has dissolved and the mixture is just warm to the touch. Remove the bowl from the pan and, using an electric mixer, whisk the eggs for 5 minutes on high speed, then reduce the speed to medium and whisk for a further 3 minutes. At this stage the mixture should form a very thick, slowly dissolving ribbon when the whisk is lifted from the bowl.

3. Sift the flour over the egg mixture and gently fold together, trying to keep as much volume as possible. Pour the cake batter into the prepared tin and lightly tap on the work surface to level out. Bake for 25–30 minutes, or until it springs back when lightly touched. Allow the cake to cool in the tin for 10 minutes before turning out onto a wire rack to cool completely.

4. Repeat with the remaining mixtures using the appropriate tin sizes (23cm for the large cakes and 15cm for the small cakes). For the chocolate layers, whisk the cocoa powder and flour together, then sift the mixture over the egg mixture. Bake the 23cm cakes for 25–30 minutes and the 15cm cakes for 15–20 minutes, or until a skewer inserted into the middle of the cake comes out clean.

5. To make the buttercream, put 160ml water and the sugar into a pan over medium heat, and have a sugar thermometer ready. Put the egg whites into a clean, grease-free bowl (this is best done using a freestanding electric mixer). As the syrup reaches about 115°C, start whisking the eggs on high speed.

6. Cook until the syrup registers 121°C, then remove from the heat and, with the mixer still running, pour the syrup in a slow stream down the side of the bowl containing the whites, avoiding the beaters. Continue whisking on high speed until the meringue is at room temperature.

7. With the mixer on medium–high, add the butter, a few pieces at a time, beating until fully combined. When adding the butter it can sometimes look curdled; if this happens, don't worry, just keep mixing and eventually it will smooth out again forming a light buttercream. Add the jam and mix to combine.

8. To make the simple syrup, put the sugar, vanilla and 150ml water into a small pan over high heat. Bring to the boil, then reduce the temperature and simmer for a few minutes until reduced slightly. Take the pan off the heat and set aside until needed.

9. To assemble the cake, use a serrated knife to cut each cake into three equal layers. Put a layer of either the large vanilla or chocolate cake onto the large cardboard cake drum or cake stand and brush with a layer of syrup. Top with a thin layer of the buttercream, spreading it so that it just peeks over the edge. Repeat the process, alternating the colours of the layers until all the larger cake layers are used.

10. Push the dowelling rods into the cake about 9cm from the outer edge, in a triangle shape. Mark where the rods are level with the cake and then remove and cut them so that they sit flush with the top. Put the 15cm cardboard cake round onto the large cake, sitting it on the dowels. Repeat the layering process with the 15cm cakes and finish the cake by arranging the strawberries around the edges and on top of the cake.

TIP

It's an exceptionally light sponge, but it is not intended to be stored. Make the cake as close to the wedding as possible, and no earlier than two days beforehand.

Macaron Tower

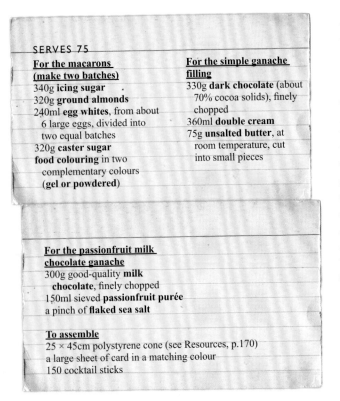

SERVES 75

For the macarons
(make two batches)
340g **icing sugar** .
320g **ground almonds**
240ml **egg whites**, from about
  6 large eggs, divided into
  two equal batches
320g **caster sugar**
food colouring in two
  complementary colours
  (gel or powdered)

For the simple ganache
filling
330g **dark chocolate** (about
  70% cocoa solids), finely
  chopped
360ml **double cream**
75g **unsalted butter**, at
  room temperature, cut
  into small pieces

For the passionfruit milk
chocolate ganache
300g good-quality **milk**
  chocolate, finely chopped
150ml sieved **passionfruit purée**
a pinch of **flaked sea salt**

To assemble
25 × 45cm polystyrene cone (see Resources, p.170)
a large sheet of card in a matching colour
150 cocktail sticks

A macaron tower is about a million miles away from a traditional white wedding cake. You can be totally creative with the colours and flavours, and by making it yourself it will be significantly cheaper than buying a wedding cake. This recipe will take time, but you can make the batches of macarons over a week and then assemble them on the day. The effort will be worth it, because it will look spectacular. I have provided a simple dark chocolate ganache recipe for the filling as well as a passionfruit milk chocolate ganache, but you can use any flavoured ganache if you prefer. Be creative – make the tower the way you want it to be for your special day.

1. You need to make two batches of macarons using the quantities given above for each batch, each using a different food colouring. Each batch requires five or six baking sheets. If you don't have that many, you can halve the recipe and make four batches instead (two in each of the colours).

2. Line five or six baking sheets with baking parchment. Put the icing sugar and ground almonds into the bowl of a food processor and pulse about 15 times until fully combined. Sift this mixture into a large bowl, discarding any small particles that remain in the sieve.

3. Add the first batch of egg whites to the almond mixture, and mix together to form a thick paste. Set aside.

4. Put 100ml water and the caster sugar into a small pan over medium heat. Bring to the boil and have a sugar thermometer ready. Meanwhile, put the remaining egg whites into a clean, grease-free bowl (this is best done using a freestanding electric mixer). Start whisking the whites on high speed when the syrup in the pan reaches about 110°C on the sugar thermometer. Cook until the syrup registers 118°C. With the mixer still running, pour the syrup in a slow stream down the side of the bowl containing the whites, avoiding the whisk.

5. Continue to whisk the meringue on high speed until the mixture has cooled and the bowl is no longer hot to the touch but is still a little warm. Add the food colouring and whisk to combine.

6. Scrape the meringue onto the almond mixture and gently fold together. It is important at this stage not to over-mix the batter. The batter should fall in a thick ribbon from the spatula, fading back into the batter within about 30 seconds. If it doesn't, fold a few more times.

7. Add half the batter to a piping bag fitted with a large round piping tip. Pipe rounds about 2.5cm in diameter onto the prepared baking sheets, repeating with the remaining batter. Leave to rest for 30 minutes or until the macarons have developed a skin and are no longer sticky. Preheat the oven to 170°C (150°C fan oven) mark 3.

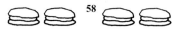

8. Bake the macarons for 12 minutes. Immediately, slide the baking parchment onto the work surface and allow to cool for a few minutes before gently peeling the macarons off the paper. Leave to cool completely. Repeat steps 2–8 to make second batch of macarons.

9. To make the simple ganache, put the chocolate into a medium heatproof bowl and set aside. Put the cream into a small pan over medium heat and bring just to the boil. Pour over the chocolate and allow to stand for a few minutes before stirring gently to form a silky smooth ganache.

10. Add the butter and gently stir until just smooth and combined. Allow the filling to stand until thickened enough to pipe.

11. For the passionfruit milk chocolate ganache, put the chocolate into a medium heatproof bowl and set aside. Put the passionfruit purée and the salt into a medium pan, then put over medium heat and bring to the boil. Pour over the chocolate and allow to stand for a few minutes before stirring gently to combine. Allow to stand until thick enough to pipe; this ganache will take longer to thicken than the simple ganache.

12. Fill a piping bag fitted with a small plain piping tip with one of the ganaches and pipe onto half the macaron shells of one colour. Sandwich with another macaron shell in the same colour. Repeat with the other ganache and the other shells. (In the tower pictured I filled the purple with the simple ganache and the yellow with the passionfruit.) You can prepare the macarons ahead, if you like: freeze for up to one month or chill for up to five days.

13. To assemble the tower, wrap the polystyrene cone neatly with the card (this is so that when the macarons are removed there won't be any polystyrene showing). To stick the macarons to the tower, push a cocktail stick through the card into the polystyrene at a 45-degree angle leaving about 1.5cm protruding. As you get nearer the top of the tower you will need to cut the cocktail sticks in half so that they don't poke out of the other side. Gently press the macaron onto the cocktail stick, making sure it doesn't poke through the front of the macaron. (The recipe should give you a few macarons extra in case any break or don't turn out successfully.)

14. To make the swirl pattern, use alternate colours of macarons, and when you start a new row put the macarons between the ones on the row below. Because it is unlikely that all your macarons will be perfectly the same size, decide which part of the cone you would like to be at the front, and then finish each row on the opposite side of the cone. This way any imperfections will be hidden on the back.

TIP

If making this for a wedding, assemble the cake on site as it is delicate and is best not moved once prepared.

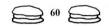

Wedding Cheesecake

SERVES 40

For the large (23cm) cheesecake
225g **digestive biscuits**
110g **unsalted butter**, melted
900g **full-fat cream cheese**
450g **caster sugar**
1 tbsp **plain flour**
4 large **eggs**, lightly beaten
1 tsp **vanilla bean paste**

For the small (15cm) cheesecake
100g **digestive biscuits**
50g **unsalted butter**, melted
450g **full-fat cream cheese**
25g **caster sugar**
1 tbsp **plain flour**
2 large **eggs**, lightly beaten
1 tsp **vanilla bean paste**

To finish
23cm and 15cm cardboard cake rounds
4 plastic or wooden dowelling rods
fresh flowers or fruit
ribbon (optional)

This is a small wedding cake that is perfect for a couple who wants something a little different. Many people don't like traditional wedding cakes, so it seems wasteful to spend hundreds of pounds on something that looks lovely but that people won't enjoy eating. This cake is ridiculously cheap in comparison to something more traditional, so it's also great for those watching the budget. Although this two-tiered cake is simple to achieve, you could, of course, increase the number of tiers; my boyfriend's sister has asked me to make her a 12-tiered cheesecake for her wedding – wish me luck!

1. For the large cheesecake, preheat the oven to 180°C (160°C fan oven) mark 4 and line the base of a 23cm springform cake tin with baking parchment. Put the digestive biscuits into a medium bowl and, using the base of rolling pin, crush them into fine crumbs. Add the melted butter and stir to coat evenly.

2. Firmly press the mixture into the base and a little up the sides of the prepared tin. Bake for 10 minutes, then remove from the oven and allow to cool while you make the filling. Reduce the oven temperature to 150°C (130°C fan oven) mark 2.

3. In the bowl of a freestanding electric mixer fitted with the paddle attachment, or using a electric mixer, beat the cream cheese until smooth and creamy, about 3 minutes. Add the sugar and flour, and beat until combined – the less you beat a baked cheesecake mixture the better; if you over-beat, the cake will have a higher chance of developing cracks.

4. Beat in the eggs and vanilla paste, a little at a time, beating until just fully combined. Pour onto the biscuit base and level out with a spatula. Bake for 1½ hours or until the edges are set but the centre is still wobbly. Cool completely before chilling for 8 hours or until ready to serve.

5. Repeat to make the small cheesecake using a 15cm springform cake tin and baking it for about 1 hour.

6. Once the cakes are thoroughly chilled you can assemble the cake. Put the large cake onto a 23cm cardboard cake round and press 4 dowelling rods in a square formation about 6.5cm from the outer edge, then mark where they are flush with the top of the cake. Now remove the dowels and cut them to fit, then push them back inside the cake. Put the small cake onto a 15cm cardboard cake round and put this in the centre of the larger cake, resting it on the dowels.

7. To decorate, put fresh flowers or fruit around the middle and on the top. If you want to make the cake look a little more traditional, you can also wrap the sides of the cakes with a piece of ribbon. Because the edge of the cake is moist, you will need to use a few layers of ribbon to make sure that no moisture bleeds through.

61

Wedding Cake Cookies

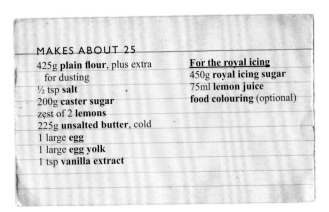

MAKES ABOUT 25

425g **plain flour**, plus extra for dusting
½ tsp **salt**
200g **caster sugar**
zest of 2 **lemons**
225g **unsalted butter**, cold
1 large **egg**
1 large **egg yolk**
1 tsp **vanilla extract**

For the royal icing
450g **royal icing sugar**
75ml **lemon juice**
food colouring (optional)

These cookies are very cute and would make a really personal favour for any wedding. Although I have made the icing white, you could colour the icing with a few drops of food colouring, and this way you can match the decoration of the cookies to the theme or style of the wedding. See page 168 for the template.

1. Line two baking sheets with baking parchment. Put the flour, salt, sugar and lemon zest in the bowl of a food processor and pulse to combine. Add the butter and pulse until the mixture resembles coarse breadcrumbs. (Alternatively, mix the dry ingredients in a large bowl and rub the butter into the flour by hand or using a pastry cutter.) Add the egg, yolk and vanilla extract and pulse, or stir, until the mixture just comes together. Tip onto a lightly floured work surface and gently knead together until uniform. Divide the dough in half and wrap in clingfilm, then chill for about 1 hour.

2. Remove the dough from the fridge and allow to rest for 10 minutes before rolling out. Working with one half of the dough at a time, roll out to a thickness of 4–5mm. Using a wedding cake-shaped cookie cutter or template (see page 168), cut out as many cookies as possible. Re-roll the scraps to cut out more biscuits. Lift the cookies off the surface with a spatula and put onto the baking sheet. Chill for 15–20 minutes. Meanwhile, preheat the oven to 180°C (160°C fan oven) mark 4.

3. Bake the cookies for 15–18 minutes or until the edges turn golden. Allow to cool on the baking sheets for 10 minutes before transferring to a wire rack to cool completely.

4. To make the royal icing put the royal icing sugar into a large bowl and add the lemon juice. Using a wooden spoon, mix gently to incorporate the two together. Once combined, beat the mixture until you have a thick and smooth paste. If you want to colour the icing, add a few drops of your chosen colour.

5. To decorate the cookies, put the icing into a piping bag fitted with a thin plain piping tube, about 2mm wide. Pipe the icing around the outline of the cookies and then pipe on your decorations. You can pipe whatever decoration comes to mind; one of the simplest is a crosshatch pattern. Once decorated, allow the icing to dry for a few hours.

TIP

If you would like your cookies to have a bit of glam, sprinkle some edible glitter or coloured sugar onto the icing while it is still wet to add a bit of sparkle.

Salted Caramel Truffles

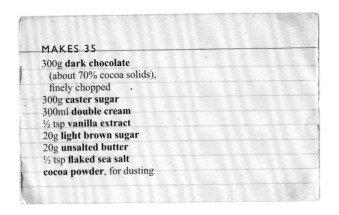

MAKES 35

300g **dark chocolate**
  (about 70% cocoa solids),
  finely chopped
300g **caster sugar**
300ml **double cream**
½ tsp **vanilla extract**
20g **light brown sugar**
20g **unsalted butter**
½ tsp **flaked sea salt**
cocoa powder, for dusting

The flavours of salted caramel and chocolate make a delicious combination. These truffles are super-easy to prepare and would make perfect favours for a wedding, so much better than the boring classic choice of sugared almonds – and homemade is always so much more special than bought.

1. Put the chocolate in a medium heatproof bowl and set aside. Put the caster sugar in a medium pan over medium heat and leave until the sugar begins to dissolve and caramelise around the edges. Using a silicon spatula, drag the dissolved sugar towards the middle to help it dissolve evenly.

2. Once the sugar is fully dissolved and has turned a dark golden brown colour, pour in half the cream, and all the vanilla and light brown sugar, it will bubble up furiously, so be careful and go slowly. Once the bubbling has subsided, add the remaining cream. If the caramel is lumpy, put over low heat and allow to melt. Once you have a smooth caramel, add the butter and sea salt, and stir gently to combine.

3. Pour the hot caramel over the chocolate and gently stir to combine. Chill until firm enough to form into balls.

4. To make the truffles, have a small bowl of cocoa powder ready and a baking tray lined with baking parchment. Take large teaspoons of the ganache mixture and roll into balls, then roll in the cocoa powder and set on the baking tray. Chill the truffles until needed.

TIP

If the ganache splits when you add the caramel, use a hand blender to bring it back together.

64

Mexican Wedding Cookies

MAKES 40

225g **unsalted butter**
80g **icing sugar**
1 tsp **vanilla extract**.
280g **plain flour**, plus extra for
dusting
100g **pecans**, finely chopped
1 tsp **ground cinnamon**
½ tsp **flaked sea salt**

For the coating
100g **icing sugar**
1 tsp **ground cinnamon**

These cookies go by many different names, including Russian tea cakes and butterballs. Normally they are made in the same way as most cookies and are domed and look like snowballs (which is another name for them), but as wedding favours I think they look a little more elegant rolled and cut into rounds. The cookies are covered in icing sugar and cinnamon after baking.

1. Line two baking sheets with baking parchment. Put the butter, icing sugar and vanilla into the bowl of a food processor and pulse until smooth and creamy. Add the flour, pecans, cinnamon and salt, and pulse until evenly combined. (Alternatively, beat together the butter, icing sugar and vanilla, then stir in the flour, pecan nuts, cinnamon and salt until fully combined.) Tip the dough onto a lightly floured work surface and form into a round. Wrap with clingfilm and chill for 30 minutes.

2. Dust the work surface with a little flour and roll out the dough until it is about 4mm thick. Cut out rounds using a 5cm cookie cutter. Place on the prepared baking sheet and chill for 15 minutes or until firm. Preheat the oven to 180°C (160°C fan oven) mark 4.

3. Bake the cookies for 12–14 minutes or until the edges are golden brown. Allow to cool on the tray for 10 minutes before transferring to a wire rack to cool.

4. Meanwhile, make the coating. Mix the icing sugar and cinnamon together in a small bowl. When the cookies are no longer hot but still slightly warm, coat them in the icing sugar mixture. Stored in a sealed container, these cookies will keep well for about four days.

Apple Strudel

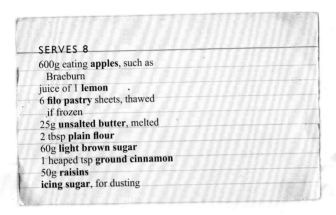

SERVES 8

600g eating **apples**, such as
   Braeburn
juice of 1 **lemon**
6 **filo pastry** sheets, thawed
   if frozen
25g **unsalted butter**, melted
2 tbsp **plain flour**
60g **light brown sugar**
1 heaped tsp **ground cinnamon**
50g **raisins**
icing sugar, for dusting

Apple strudel is one of those dishes that I hadn't eaten for years until recently, although it was a firm favourite when I was little, and I seem to remember eating it at my friends' houses a lot when I was a kid. Technically, this isn't a genuine strudel, because it doesn't use strudel pastry but, frankly, as much as I love making pastry, strudel dough isn't the easiest to use; it has to be stretched wafer thin using your hands, and although it is delicious I am happy using shop-bought filo pastry for a fast and tasty homemade version.

1. Preheat the oven to 190°C (170°C fan oven) mark 5 and line a baking sheet with baking parchment. Peel and core the apples, then slice them into thin wedges and put them into a large bowl with the lemon juice. This will stop the apples from browning.

2. Put a sheet of filo pastry on the prepared baking sheet and brush lightly with the melted butter (cover the unused pastry with a damp tea towel). Cover with a second sheet of filo and repeat the process until all six sheets have been used.

3. Drain the lemon juice from the apples and toss with the plain flour, sugar, cinnamon and raisins. Put the apple mixture along the long edge of the pastry and roll up to form the strudel, squeezing the ends together to seal. Bake for 30–40 minutes or until the pastry is crisp and golden. Allow to cool slightly, then dust with a little icing sugar before serving.

CHAPTER TWO: ROMANCE

Springtime Blossom Cake

SERVES 12

300g **unsalted butter**, at room temperature, plus extra for greasing
300g **caster sugar**
5 large **eggs**, lightly beaten
2 tsp **vanilla extract**
300g **self-raising flour**
100g **soured cream**

For the vanilla buttercream
250g **unsalted butter**, at room temperature
100ml **double cream**

1 tsp **vanilla bean paste**
550g **icing sugar**
pinch of **salt**

To finish
80g **raspberry jam**
icing sugar, for dusting
600g **white sugarpaste**
100g **peach sugarpaste**
100g **violet sugarpaste**
a little **royal icing**
nonpareils (optional)

This cake is simple to put together, but the decoration does take a little time. It's perfect to show your loved one that you have put in a bit of effort! To help create level layers, make sure the cake is fully cooled, and then chill in the fridge for 10 minutes, as this will lead to fewer crumbs when slicing the cake into halves. Make sure all the cake ingredients are at room temperature, so they will blend together more easily and create a lighter cake.

1. Preheat the oven to 180°C (160°C fan oven) mark 4, then grease and line a deep 23cm cake tin with baking parchment, greasing the parchment too. Put the butter into a large bowl and, using an electric mixer, beat until smooth and creamy, about 3 minutes. Add the sugar and beat until light and fluffy, about 5 minutes.

2. Add the eggs, a little at a time, beating well after each addition and scraping down the bowl when needed. Once the eggs are fully incorporated, add the vanilla extract and half the flour, and beat until just combined. Add the soured cream and mix to combine, then add the remaining flour and beat until fully combined, but be careful not to over-mix.

3. Pour the batter into the prepared tin and bake for 1 hour 20 minutes or until the cake springs back when lightly touched or a skewer inserted into the centre comes out clean. Allow the cake to cool in the tin for 20 minutes before turning out onto a wire rack to cool completely.

4. To make the buttercream, put the butter into a large bowl and, using an electric mixer, beat until light and creamy, about 3 minutes. Slowly pour in the cream and add the vanilla paste, mixing until fully combined. Add the icing sugar and salt, a little at a time, beating until fully combined. Once the sugar is fully incorporated, turn the mixer to high and beat until the buttercream is light and fluffy.

5. To assemble the cake, put the cake onto a cardboard cake board or serving plate. If the cake is domed, use a serrated knife to level it, then slice the cake in half. Spread jam on the base cake. On the base of the top half of cake spread a thick layer of buttercream. Sandwich the layers together, then cover the top and sides of the cake with a smooth layer of buttercream.

6. To decorate, dust a clean work surface with a small amount of icing sugar, and knead the white sugarpaste until pliable. Roll the paste until it is large enough to cover the cake. The easiest way to do this is to take a piece of string and use it as a guide. Drape it over the cake and grip it where it meets the table. Lift the string from the cake and use this as a measure for your sugarpaste. Using the flats of your hands and arms, drape the sugarpaste over the cake and use the palms of your hands to smooth the top, applying gentle pressure. Carefully work your way around the cake, gently smoothing the sugarpaste onto the sides, trimming off the excess.

7. To create the decorations, roll the peach and violet sugarpastes until thin and, using different-sized blossom cutters, press out as many flowers as you can. To give the flowers some body, put each into your palm and gently press in the centre of the flower. This keeps them from being completely flat and gives the cake more visual appeal.

8. If you want to go a step further, you can add a white nonpareil to the centre of each, gently pressing it into the sugarpaste. Allow the flowers to dry out for 2 hours before attaching them to the cake. To stick the flowers to the cake, pipe a small amount of royal icing to the back of the flowers and gently stick them to the cake.

68

Orange & Chocolate
50th Anniversary Cake

SERVES 12

225g **unsalted butter** at room temperature, plus extra for greasing	300ml **buttermilk**
325g **plain flour**	**edible gold powder**, to decorate
50g **cornflour**	
4½ tsp **baking powder**	**For the orange Italian meringue buttercream**
½ tsp **salt**	250g **caster sugar**
350g **caster sugar**	6 medium **egg whites**
zest of 2 large **oranges**	450g **unsalted butter** at room temperature
1 tsp **vanilla extract**	350g **orange curd**
4 medium **eggs**	

For the chocolate glaze
150g **dark chocolate** (about 70% cocoa solids)
200ml double cream

I have very strong memories of my grandparents' 50th anniversary. The whole family got together and we had a party. For presents, we bought 50 gifts, some just silly little things but each and every one was related to gold, the traditional gift for a 50th anniversary. There was everything from a gold photo frame to gold-wrapped chocolates. If only we had served this golden cake, everything would have been tinged with gold.

1. Preheat the oven to 180°C (160°C fan oven) mark 4, then grease and line three 20cm cake tins with baking parchment, greasing the parchment too. In a medium bowl whisk the flour, cornflour, baking powder and salt together to combine, then set aside.

2. Put the butter into a large bowl. Using an electric mixer, beat the butter on medium–high speed until smooth and light, add the sugar and orange zest and beat until light and fluffy, about 5 minutes. Add the vanilla and mix to combine. With the mixer on medium speed, beat in the eggs, a little at a time, beating until fully combined before adding the next. With the mixer on low, add the flour mixture in three additions, alternating with the buttermilk, starting and finishing with the flour. Divide the batter between the prepared tins and bake for 25–30 minutes or until the cakes are golden brown and spring back when lightly touched. Allow to cool in the tins for 10 minutes before turning out onto wire racks to cool completely.

3. To make the meringue buttercream, put 60ml water and the sugar into a pan over medium heat. Bring to the boil and have a sugar thermometer ready. Meanwhile, put the egg whites into a clean, grease-free bowl (this is best done using a freestanding electric mixer). Start whisking the whites on high speed when the syrup in the pan reaches about 115°C on the sugar thermometer. Cook until the syrup registers 121°C. With the mixer still running, pour the syrup in a slow stream down the side of the bowl containing the whites, avoiding the beaters. Continue whisking on high speed until the meringue is at room temperature.

4. With the mixer on medium–high speed, add the butter, a few pieces at a time, beating until fully combined. When adding the butter it can sometimes look curdled; don't worry, just keep mixing and eventually it will smooth out to form a light buttercream. Add 250g of the orange curd and mix until fully combined.

5. To assemble the cake, put the first cake layer onto a cardboard cake round, cake stand or serving plate and top with a layer of buttercream. Add half the remaining orange curd and repeat the process with the second layer of cake, finishing with the final layer of cake. Use the remaining buttercream to coat the top and sides. Using a long offset spatula, smooth the buttercream so that the tops and sides are perfectly smooth. Put the cake in the fridge for 15 minutes while you make the glaze.

6. Put the chocolate into a medium heatproof bowl and set aside. Put the cream in a small pan over medium heat. When the cream comes to the boil remove from the heat and pour over the chocolate. Allow to stand for a couple of minutes before stirring together to form a silky smooth ganache. Pour the ganache over the chilled cake, teasing it over the edges so that it drips down the buttercream. Before the ganache fully sets, dip a small paintbrush into edible gold powder and flick the powder over the chocolate to give the cake a golden shimmer.

festive

S'mores Cake

SERVES 12

225g **unsalted** butter, at room temperature, plus extra for greasing	2 tsp **vanilla extract**
325g **plain flour**	4 medium **eggs**, lightly beaten
50g **cornflour**	300ml **whole milk**
2 tsp **ground cinnamon**	
4½ tsp **baking powder**	
½ tsp **salt**	
350g **caster sugar**	

For the whipped ganache filling	**For the Swiss meringue**
75g **dark chocolate** (about 70% cocoa solids), finely chopped	160g **egg whites** (about 4 large eggs)
115g **double cream**	380g caster sugar
10g **light brown sugar**	½ tsp cream of tartar

When I was a child I was a scout, and although it wasn't really my thing, one of the few activities that I really did enjoy was the campfires and roasted marshmallows served between digestive biscuits. This simple treat is perfectly delicious as it is, but it was taken a step further across the pond when they added chocolate – and everything is better with chocolate! As the name suggests, you will always want s'more!

1. Preheat the oven to 180°C (160°C fan oven) mark 4, then grease and line three 20cm round cake tins with baking parchment, greasing the parchment too. In a medium bowl whisk the flour, cornflour, cinnamon, baking powder and salt together to combine, then set aside.

2. Put the butter into a large bowl. Using an electric mixer, beat the butter on medium–high speed until smooth and light, add the sugar and beat until light and fluffy, about 5 minutes. Add the vanilla and mix to combine. With the mixer on medium speed, add the eggs, a little at a time, beating until fully combined before adding more. With the mixer on low, add the flour mixture in three additions, alternating with the milk, starting and finishing with the flour.

3. Divide the batter evenly among the prepared tins and bake for 30–35 minutes or until the cake is golden brown and springs back when lightly touched. Allow the cakes to cool in the tins for 10 minutes before turning out onto a wire rack to cool completely.

4. To make the ganache filling, put the chocolate into a medium heatproof bowl. Put the cream and sugar into a small pan over medium heat and bring just to the boil. Immediately, pour the hot cream over the chocolate and allow to stand for a few minutes before gently stirring together to form a smooth silky ganache. Chill the ganache until cool and slightly thickened, but not set. Using a whisk, beat until thickened. Spread the ganache across two of the cake layers and set aside while you make the Swiss meringue.

5. Put the egg whites, sugar and cream of tartar into a heatproof bowl set over a pan of gently simmering water, and whisk constantly until the sugar has dissolved and the egg whites are warm to the touch. Remove the bowl from the heat and, using an electric mixer, whisk until the meringue forms stiff glossy peaks. (When you have made the meringue, you need to work with it fairly quickly. Don't allow it to stand or it will firm up too much to spread easily.)

6. To assemble the cake, put the first cake layer topped with chocolate onto a cake stand or serving plate and spread with a thin layer of the meringue. Repeat with the second chocolate-topped cake layer and finish with the final layer. Take the remaining meringue and spread across the top and sides of the cake – this doesn't have to look perfect, as any imperfections will just add to the effect. To finish the cake, take a blowtorch and lightly torch the meringue until it is golden.

Pecan Pie Cake

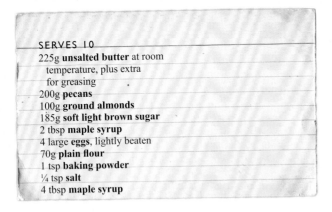

SERVES 10

225g **unsalted butter** at room
   temperature, plus extra
   for greasing
200g **pecans**
100g **ground almonds**
185g **soft light brown sugar**
2 tbsp **maple syrup**
4 large **eggs**, lightly beaten
70g **plain flour**
1 tsp **baking powder**
¼ tsp **salt**
4 tbsp **maple syrup**

I love pecan pie. It is one of those seasonal dishes that I could happily eat all year round. Sometimes I want something a little less sugary and easier to make than the pie, and this cake is just that recipe – perfect for a lazy weekend treat. The simple cake is made with ground almonds and pecans with the warm flavour of maple syrup.

1. Preheat the oven to 180°C (160°C fan oven) mark 4. Lightly grease and line a deep 20cm cake tin with baking parchment, greasing the parchment too. Put the pecans on a baking tray and put in the oven to toast for 5 minutes or until fragrant. Watch the nuts carefully, as they burn easily.

2. Put half the pecans and all the ground almonds into the bowl of a food processor and pulse until they are fairly fine. You won't get the pecans as fine as the almonds but that doesn't matter.

3. Put the butter into a large bowl and, using an electric mixer, beat until light and creamy, about 3 minutes. Add the light brown sugar and maple syrup and beat until light and fluffy, about 5 minutes. Add the eggs, a little a time, beating until fully combined. Sift the flour, baking powder and salt into the bowl with the nuts and mix to combine evenly. Add this mixture to the butter mixture and fold to combine. Pour the batter into the prepared tin and gently level out.

4. Bake for 50–55 minutes or until the cake is golden brown and springs backs when lightly touched. If the cake browns too quickly, put a tent of foil over the top.

5. While the cake is baking, make the topping by roughly chopping the remaining pecans and mixing them with the maple syrup. Remove the cake from the oven and cool in the tin for 10 minutes before turning out onto a wire rack. Sprinkle the topping over the cake and allow to cool before serving.

CHAPTER THREE: THANKSGIVING

Salted Caramel Apple Pie

SERVES 8

500g **plain flour**, plus extra for dusting	10g **unsalted butter**
	a large pinch of **sea salt**
1 tsp **salt**	**For the apple filling**
2 tbsp **caster sugar**	1.3kg eating **apples**, such
250g **unsalted butter**, chilled and diced	as a mixture of Granny Smith and Braeburn
125–150ml ice-cold **water**	1 tsp **lemon juice**
1 large **egg** mixed with 1 tbsp water	1½ tsp **cinnamon**
	½ tsp freshly grated **nutmeg**
For the salted caramel filling	3 tbsp **cornflour**
150g **caster sugar**	
75ml **double cream**	

Apple pie is classic comfort food – and I love it – but when I heard about a bakery in New York that had added salted caramel, I knew I had to come up with my own version. The caramel recipe makes a little more than needed, but you can use it when serving the pie, along with a scoop of vanilla ice cream, of course.

1. To make the salted caramel filling, put the caster sugar in a medium pan over medium heat and leave until the sugar begins to dissolve and caramelise around the edges. Using a silicon spatula, drag the dissolved sugar towards the middle to help it dissolve evenly.

2. Once the sugar is fully dissolved and has turned a dark golden brown colour, pour in half the cream, it will bubble up furiously, so be careful and go slowly. Once the bubbling has subsided, add the remaining cream. If the caramel is lumpy, put over a low heat and allow to melt. Once you have a smooth caramel, add the butter and sea salt, and stir gently to combine. Pour the caramel into a jug to cool until needed.

3. Put the flour, salt and sugar into the bowl of a food processor and pulse to combine. Add the chilled butter and pulse until it forms small chunks, just under the size of a pea. Slowly add the water while pulsing the food processor until the pastry holds together when squeezed. (Alternatively, mix the dry ingredients in a bowl and add the butter. Rub together with your fingertips until the butter pieces are just under the size of a pea. Slowly stir in the water, using a fork, until the pastry holds together.) If you add too much water the pastry will become too soft. Tip the dough onto the work surface and gently knead together. Divide into two balls, one a little larger than the other. Wrap in clingfilm and chill for 30 minutes.

4. Lightly dust the work surface with flour and roll out the larger piece of pastry, until it is large enough to line a 23cm pie plate. Gently roll the pastry around your rolling pin, and then drape over the pie plate. Press the dough into the plate and then trim the excess leaving a 2.5cm overhang. Take the second piece of pastry and roll out as before, then put the pastry on a baking sheet. Chill the lined pie plate and the rolled pastry while you make the filling.

5. Peel, core and slice the apples, adding them to a large bowl with the lemon juice to prevent browning. Add the cinnamon, nutmeg and cornflour, and toss together to coat evenly.

6. To assemble the pie, remove the pastry from the fridge and place a third of the apples into the lined pie plate. Top with about a quarter of the caramel and then repeat the process with the remaining two-thirds of the apples. Brush the pastry overhang with a little of the egg wash (the egg and water mixed together) and then drape the remaining pastry on top of the pie.

7. Trim the excess, leaving you with a 2.5cm overhang. Roll the excess pastry under itself to form the pie's edge. To crimp the pie, pinch together the thumb and forefinger of one hand against the edge of the pie crust and, using the index finger of the other, press the pastry together along the top edge to form a simple scallop. Chill the prepared pie for 30 minutes before baking. Preheat the oven to 200°C (180°C fan oven) mark 6.

8. Brush the pie with egg wash and, using a sharp knife, cut a few vent holes in the top of the pastry. Bake for 10 minutes, then reduce the temperature to 190°C (170°C fan oven) mark 5 and bake for a further 1 hour or until the pastry is golden and the filling is bubbling. If the pastry is browning too fast, put a tent of foil over the top. Allow to cool before serving.

77

Cherry Pie

SERVES 8

200g **caster sugar**
800g pitted or frozen **cherries**
zest and juice of 1 **lemon**
45g **cornflour**

For the pastry
400g **plain flour**, plus extra
    for dusting
1 tsp **salt**
2 tbsp **caster sugar**

200g **unsalted butter**,
    diced and chilled
100–125ml ice-cold **water**
1 medium **egg**, beaten
    with 1 tbsp **water**

To my mind cherry pie is one of those desserts that is quintessentially American. Because cherries can be quite watery, I make the filling in a pan. This helps to lower the risk of a watery filling, which would make the pastry soggy. As the season for fresh cherries is fairly short, I normally make this with frozen cherries so that I can have the pie all year round.

1. Put the sugar, 600g of the cherries and the lemon zest into a large pan over medium heat. Put the cornflour and lemon juice into a small bowl and mix to form a smooth paste. As the cherries begin to release their juice, add this paste to the pan and cook the cherries gently, stirring, until the juice comes to the boil. Cook, stirring, for a few more minutes until thickened. Remove from the heat and add the reserved cherries. Set aside to cool while you make the pastry.

2. Put the flour, salt and sugar into the bowl of a food processor and pulse to combine. Add the chilled butter and pulse until it forms small chunks, just under the size of a pea. Slowly add the water while pulsing the food processor until the pastry holds together when squeezed. (Alternatively, mix the dry ingredients in a bowl and add the butter. Rub together with your fingertips until the butter pieces are just under the size of a pea. Slowly stir in the water, using a fork, until the pastry holds together.) If you add too much water the pastry will be too soft. Tip the dough onto the work surface and gently knead together. Divide into two balls, one a little larger than the other. Wrap in clingfilm and chill for 30 minutes.

3. Lightly dust the work surface with flour and roll out the larger piece of pastry, until it is large enough to line a 23cm pie plate. Gently roll the pastry around your rolling pin, and then drape it over the pie plate. Press the dough into the plate and then trim the excess leaving a 2.5cm overhang. Take the second piece of pastry and roll out as before. Using a knife or pizza cutter, cut the pastry into strips 2.5cm thick. Put the pie plate and the strips of pastry into the fridge for 15 minutes to let the pastry rest.

4. Preheat the oven to 200°C (180°C fan oven) mark 6. Remove the pie plate and strips of pastry from the fridge and tip the filling into the prepared base. Brush the edge of the pie and the overhang with a little egg and water wash, and then lay half the pastry strips over the pie. Brush the strips with egg, then put the second half of strips at a 90-degree angle from the first half creating a very simple lattice pattern. As before, brush the lattice with egg wash.

5. To finish the pie, fold the pastry overhang so that it sits on the rim of the plate and covers the edges of the pastry strips. To crimp the pie, pinch together the thumb and forefinger of one hand against the edge of the pie crust and, using the index finger of the other, press the pastry together along the top edge to form a simple scallop. Bake for 40–45 minutes or until the pastry is golden and the filling is bubbling.

Crêpe Cake

SERVES 8

150g **plain flour**
2 tbsp **caster sugar**
¼ tsp **salt**
2 large **eggs**
150ml **whole milk**
25g **unsalted butter**, melted
 and cooled
vegetable oil, for greasing
icing sugar, for dusting

For the filling
300ml **double cream**
100g **lemon curd**
200g **raspberry jam**

Sometimes you don't want a layered cake but something different and lighter. This crêpe cake is easy to prepare and would make a lovely Eastertime dessert. I have filled it with lemon and jam, but you could use other ingredients such as chocolate cream and pistachios, perhaps – whatever you fancy.

1. Put the flour, sugar and salt into a large bowl and whisk together, then make a well in the centre. In a medium bowl whisk together the eggs, milk and 150ml water, then pour this into the flour mixture and whisk together until smooth. Pour in the melted butter and whisk to combine. Cover the bowl with clingfilm and chill for 1 hour before cooking.

2. To cook the crêpes, lightly grease a 20cm frying pan with vegetable oil and heat the pan over medium–high heat. When the pan is hot, pour a small ladleful of the batter into the centre of the pan and swirl gently to spread it evenly across the surface.

3. Cook until the crêpe begins to brown around the edge, then flip it over and cook for a few more minutes on the other side until lightly golden. When cooked, pile the crêpes onto a sheet of baking parchment to cool while you make the rest. Repeat with the remaining batter – you should have about 12 crêpes.

4. To make the filling, lightly whisk the double cream in a large bowl until it holds soft peaks. Add the lemon curd and whisk until combined and the cream is light and fluffy.

5. To assemble the cake, put the first crêpe onto a serving plate or cake stand and spread with a layer of the lemon cream. Top with a second pancake and spread this with a thin layer of jam. Repeat this process, layering up the pancakes until you have a towering stack. You can serve immediately or, if you prefer a slightly firmer filling, chill for 1 hour. Before serving, dust with a little icing sugar.

80

Chocolate Orange Hot Cross Buns

MAKES 8

450g **strong white bread flour**, plus extra for dusting	60g **raisins**
½ tsp **salt**	60g **dark chocolate** (about 70% cocoa solids), roughly chopped
2 tsp **mixed spice**	**oil**, for greasing
50g **caster sugar**	
7g **fast-action yeast**	
zest of 1 **orange**	**For the crosses**
1 large **egg**	50g **strong white bread flour**
200ml **whole milk**, lukewarm	2 tbsp **golden syrup**, warmed
30g **unsalted butter**, melted and cooled	

For me hot cross buns shout out 'Easter!': the smell, the taste and the nostalgia of them. And while I do love the classic, my little twist makes them even more delicious by adding some dark chocolate to the dough. If you prefer the classic and want to omit the chocolate, increase the raisins to 120g and add 1 tsp ground cinnamon.

1. Line a baking sheet with baking parchment. Sift the flour, salt, mixed spice and sugar into a large bowl and add the yeast and orange zest. In a small bowl mix the egg, milk and melted butter together until combined, then tip into the flour mixture. Using a rounded knife or your hands, mix together to make a soft dough.

2. Lightly flour the work surface and tip the dough onto it. Knead the dough for 5 minutes or until it is smooth and elastic. Flatten the dough, then sprinkle over the raisins and chocolate. Fold the dough over to seal the chocolate and raisins inside, then knead for 2 minutes to evenly distribute them. Form into a ball, put into a lightly oiled bowl and cover with clingfilm. Put in a warm place and leave to rise for 1 hour or until doubled in size.

3. Tip the dough onto the floured work surface and lightly knead to knock out some of the air. Divide the dough into eight equal pieces and form into balls. Put the balls onto the baking sheet about 5cm apart. Lightly cover with clingfilm and leave to rise for 40 minutes, or until doubled in size. Meanwhile, preheat the oven to 220°C (200°C fan oven) mark 7.

4. To make the cross, put the flour and 4 tbsp water into a bowl and mix to form a thick paste. Spoon the paste into a piping bag and pipe crosses on the buns. Bake for 20–25 minutes or until risen and golden. While still warm, brush the buns with the warmed golden syrup.

Easter Nest Cupcakes

MAKES 12

225g **plain flour**	125g **unsalted butter** at
2 tsp **baking powder**	room temperature
¼ tsp **salt**	1 tbsp **double cream**
225g **unsalted butter** at	175g **icing sugar**
room temperature	pinch of **salt**
225g **caster sugar**	**For the decoration**
4 large **eggs**, lightly beaten	100g **dark chocolate**
125ml **whole milk**	(about 70% cocoa solids)
For the chocolate frosting	in one piece
110g **dark chocolate** (about	36 **mini chocolate eggs**
70% cocoa solids), finely	
chopped	

At Easter I always remember there being little Easter egg nests made of cornflakes coated in chocolate and then topped with some mini eggs. These cupcakes are a different spin on that same idea, and a perfect activity to keep kids occupied over the Easter holiday.

1. Preheat the oven to 180°C (160°C fan oven) mark 4 and line a standard 12-cup muffin pan with paper cases. In a medium bowl whisk the flour, baking powder and salt together to combine, then set aside.

2. Put the butter into a large bowl and, using an electric mixer, beat on high speed until light and creamy, about 3 minutes. Add the sugar and beat on high speed until light and fluffy, about 5 minutes.

3. Beat in the eggs, a little at a time, beating until fully combined, then add the flour mixture in three additions, alternating with the milk, starting and finishing with the flour. Divide the batter among the prepared muffin cups, and bake for 20–25 minutes or until a cocktail stick inserted into the centre of a cake comes out clean. Allow the cakes to cool in the tin for 10 minutes before transferring to a wire rack to cool completely.

4. To make the frosting, melt the chocolate in a heatproof bowl set over a pan of gently simmering water, making sure the base of the bowl doesn't touch the water. Remove from the heat and leave to cool slightly. Put the butter into a large bowl and, using an electric mixer, beat until light and smooth, about 3 minutes. Slowly incorporate the cream, then slowly add the icing sugar and salt, and beat until light and creamy. Pour in the melted chocolate and mix to combine. If the frosting is too liquid, chill for 10 minutes or until slightly thickened.

5. To decorate, spread the frosting across the tops of the cooled cupcakes and then, using a sharp knife or a vegetable peeler, grate the bar of chocolate to create shards. Scatter these over the cupcakes. Top each cake with three mini eggs to finish.

84

Simnel Cake

SERVES 12

115g **sultanas**	1 tsp **mixed spice**
115g **raisins**	170g **unsalted butter**, at
115g **currants**	room temperature
60g **mixed candied peel**	170g **caster sugar**
zest of 1 **lemon**	3 large **eggs**, lightly beaten
zest of 1 **orange**	**icing sugar**, for dusting
3 tbsp **brandy**	450g **marzipan**
170g **plain flour**	a little **apricot jam**, melted
80g **ground almonds**	and sieved
¼ tsp **salt**	1 **egg**, lightly beaten
1 tsp **ground cinnamon**	

A simnel cake is pure Easter: the meaning of the cake is based around the 12 disciples, and the 11 marzipan balls represent the 'true disciples' – Judas having been omitted. Whatever the history of the cake, it is a delicious fruit cake with a layer of marzipan baked into the centre and, as we all know from eating Christmas cake, marzipan and fruit cake are the perfect match.

1. The night before you want to make the cake, put the fruits, zests and brandy into a large bowl and mix together. Cover with clingfilm and leave to soak overnight.

2. Next day, preheat the oven to 150°C (130°C fan oven) mark 2, then grease and triple-line a deep 20cm cake tin with baking parchment. In a medium bowl whisk the flour, almonds, salt and spices together to combine, then set aside.

3. Put the butter and sugar into a large bowl and, using an electric mixer, beat until light and fluffy, about 5 minutes. Beat in the eggs, a little at a time, mixing until fully combined. With the mixer on low, add the flour mixture, a large spoonful at a time, mixing until just combined. Using a large spatula or metal spoon, fold in the fruit.

4. Dust the work surface with icing sugar and roll out a third of the marzipan, then cut it into a 20cm circle. Scrape half the batter into the prepared cake tin and level out. Put the circle of marzipan onto the cake and top with the remaining cake batter. Bake for 1¾ hours or until a cocktail stick inserted into the centre comes out clean. If the cake is browning too fast, make a tent with foil and put it over the top. Allow the cake to cool completely in the tin before removing.

5. To finish the cake, brush the top with a little melted apricot jam. Roll out half the remaining marzipan and cut out another 20cm circle. Put this on the top of the cake. Divide the remaining marzipan into 11 equal pieces and roll into balls. Using a little apricot jam as glue, stick the balls around the edge of the cake.

6. Brush the marzipan balls and disc with a little beaten egg and then, using a blowtorch, lightly brown the marzipan, or put the cake under a hot grill for 1–2 minutes.

Macadamia & Cranberry Cake

SERVES 8

75g **macadamia nuts**
50g **unsalted butter**, at
room temperature
50g **caster sugar**
1 large **egg**
35g **ground almonds**
70g **dried cranberries**
50g **white chocolate**,
roughly chopped

500g **all-butter puff
pastry**, thawed if frozen
1 large **egg**, beaten with
1 tbsp **water**

This isn't really a cake, it's a version of a French dish called 'king's cake', which is basically an almond frangipane sandwiched between layers of puff pastry. It is usually associated with Epiphany but I like it for New Year's Day. My take on this classic is a filling made with rich macadamia nuts as well as almonds, with the addition of white chocolate and cranberries. The result is creamy with hits of fruits – a lovely dish that's very easy to make.

1. Line a baking sheet with baking parchment. Grind 50g of the macadamia nuts in a food processor; be careful not to over-process them, as they will turn into nut butter if you try to grind them as finely as ground almonds. Roughly chop the remaining macadamia nuts and set aside.

2. To make the frangipane, beat the butter and sugar together until light and fluffy. Beat in the egg, a little at a time, followed by the almonds and both the ground and chopped macadamia nuts. Add the cranberries and the chocolate, and mix to combine.

3. Roll out the pastry to 3mm thick and cut out two circles 25cm in diameter. Put one circle on the prepared baking sheet and the other on a sheet of baking parchment and chill for 30 minutes. Preheat the oven to 180°C (160°C fan oven) mark 4.

4. Spread the frangipane in an even layer over the pastry round on the baking sheet, leaving a 2.5cm border. Brush the pastry border with the egg wash. Lay the second disc of pastry on top and gently press to seal the edges. Brush the cake with the egg wash, then chill the cake in the fridge for 10–15 minutes. Score the top with a knife to create a pattern. Either leave the edge plain or use a knife to create a scalloped edge. Bake for 35–40 minutes or until golden brown. Allow to cool before serving.

Vasilopita

225g **unsalted butter** at room temperature, plus extra for greasing

200g **caster sugar**

zest of 2 large **oranges**

2 tbsp **clear honey**

4 large **eggs**, lightly beaten

70g **plain flour**

1 tsp **baking powder**

¼ tsp **salt**

200g **ground almonds**

icing sugar, for dusting

gold leaf, to decorate (optional)

For the candied orange peel

2 large **oranges**

200g **caster sugar**

2–3 tbsp **Cointreau**, or to taste

This cake is my version of a classic cake served in Greece on New Year's Day. Like many other traditional cakes, a coin would have been baked into the batter and the person who found it in their slice was said to receive a year's good luck. My favourite way to decorate this simple cake is to top it with candied orange peel and a little edible gold leaf – to start the New Year in style, of course! See page 41 for how to sterilise the jars.

1. Preheat the oven to 180°C (160°C fan oven) mark 4. Lightly grease a deep 20cm cake tin with baking parchment, and grease the baking parchment. Put the butter into a large bowl and, using an electric mixer, beat until light and creamy, about 3 minutes. Add the sugar, orange zest and honey, and beat until light and fluffy, about 5 minutes.

2. Add the eggs, a little a time, beating until fully combined. Sift the flour, baking powder and salt together in a small bowl and mix in the almonds. Add this mixture to the butter mixture and fold to combine. Pour the batter into the prepared tin and gently level out.

3. Bake for 50–55 minutes until the cake is golden brown and springs backs when lightly touched. If the cake is browning too quickly, put a tent of foil over the top.

4. Meanwhile, prepare the candied peel. Using a vegetable peeler, peel off long strips of orange zest, trying to keep the slices as thin as possible so that you remove as little of the pith as possible. Cut the peel into thin strips and put them into a small pan, then cover with cold water. Put the pan over medium–high heat and bring to the boil.

5. Drain the orange peel, discarding the water, and then repeat this process twice more (this helps to reduce any bitterness in the peel). Put the sugar and 120ml water into the pan over medium–high heat and bring to the boil. Add the orange zest and then reduce the temperature so that the syrup is at a gentle simmer. Cook the orange, stirring occasionally, for 30–35 minutes or until it turns translucent. Remove from the heat and add the Cointreau. Pour the peel and syrup into a sterilised jar and seal until needed (the candied peel will last for up to three months).

6. Allow the cake to cool in the tin for 10 minutes before turning out onto a wire rack. Use a skewer to make holes all over the top of the cake. Use a pastry brush to coat the cake generously in the reserved orange syrup. Allow the cake to cool completely then dust with a little icing sugar and decorate with candied orange peel. To make the cake a little more special, I like to add a little edible gold leaf to some of the orange peel.

Hangover Cake

SERVES 8–10

55g **unsalted butter** at room temperature, plus extra for greasing 100g **plain flour** 1 tsp **baking powder** 2 tsp **ground ginger** ¼ tsp **salt** 100g **caster sugar** 1 large **egg**, lightly beaten 1 tsp **vanilla extract** 60ml **plain yogurt**	**For the topping** 50g **unsalted butter** 50g **soft light brown sugar** about 2 tbsp **dark rum** 3 large **bananas**

New Year's Day is a day of hangovers. We can all admit to enjoying the celebrations a little too much, so this is the perfect hangover cure. It's delicious, fast to make and full of things that are supposedly good for a hangover: bananas for potassium, ginger to help soothe the stomach, and a shot of rum for the hair of the dog.

1. Preheat the oven to 180°C (160°C fan oven) mark 4 and lightly grease a 20cm cake tin. To make the topping, put the butter into a small pan over medium–high heat. Once the butter has melted, add the sugar and cook until you have a smooth sauce. Take off the heat and add 2 tbsp rum. Taste the caramel, and if you want a stronger flavour, add a little more rum. Pour the caramel into the base of the prepared tin and set aside.

2. In a medium bowl whisk the flour, baking powder, ginger and salt together to combine, then set aside. Put the butter into a medium bowl and, using an electric mixer, beat until light and creamy, about 3 minutes. Add the sugar and beat together until light and fluffy, about 5 minutes. Add the egg and vanilla, a little at a time, beating until fully combined.

3. Add half the flour mixture, mixing until just combined. Mix in the yogurt, then add the remainder of the flour mixture, stirring just until combined.

4. Peel and slice the bananas into 1.5cm thick slices and spread across the base of the prepared tin, then top with the cake batter in an even layer. Bake for 25–30 minutes or until a cocktail stick inserted into the centre comes out clean. Let the cake cool in the tin for 10 minutes before inverting and turning out onto a wire rack. It is best served warm.

TIP

This makes a fairly thin cake, so if you want your cake a little taller, double the cake recipe and bake for 40–50 minutes.

Edible Flower Cupcakes

MAKES 12

225g **plain flour**	**edible fresh flowers**, such as
2 tsp **baking powder**	a mixture of **pansies, violas,**
¼ tsp **salt**	**primroses** and **rose petals,**
225g **unsalted butter,**	to decorate
at room temperature	
225g **caster sugar**	**For the frosting**
zest of 1 **lemon**	250g **unsalted butter,** at
4 large **eggs**, lightly beaten	room temperature
1 tsp **vanilla bean paste**	1 tsp **vanilla bean paste**
125ml **soured cream**	100ml **double cream**
	500g **icing sugar**, sifted
	pinch of **salt**

There are many flowers that are edible; in fact one of the most frequently used baking ingredients is derived from orchids: vanilla. So the idea of decorating cupcakes with some beautiful flowers shouldn't be that strange. Because the flavour is delicate, to allow them to shine, the cake is just lightly flavoured with vanilla and lemon, and the frosting is a beautiful smooth vanilla buttercream. When using flowers with food you need to make sure they haven't been in contact with pesticides, so use a supplier who can guarantee this (see Resources, page 170).

1. Preheat the oven to 170°C (150°C fan oven) mark 3. Line a standard 12-cup muffin pan with paper cases. In a medium bowl whisk the flour, baking powder and salt together to combine, then set aside.

2. Put the butter into a large bowl and, using an electric mixer, beat until smooth and creamy, then add the sugar and lemon zest, and beat until light and fluffy, about 5 minutes. Beat in the eggs and vanilla, a little at a time, beating well after each addition. Add the soured cream and mix until fully combined. Add the flour mixture and fold until fully combined (folding in the flour will help to prevent over-mixing).

3. Divide the batter among the cases and bake for 22–25 minutes or until a skewer inserted into one of the cakes comes out clean. Transfer to a wire rack to cool completely.

4. To make the frosting, beat the butter and vanilla bean paste using an electric mixer until light and creamy. With the mixer on medium speed, slowly incorporate the double cream. Once light and smooth, slowly incorporate the icing sugar and salt, then beat on high speed until light and fluffy.

5. To decorate the cupcakes, put the buttercream into a piping bag fitted with a large star piping tube and pipe in a spiral starting in the centre of a cupcake and working out to the edge. Take the flowers off their stems and place onto the cakes.

TIP

If you are making rose-decorated cakes, add a little rose syrup to the buttercream to add a delicate floral note.

Individual Carrot Cakes

MAKES 12

oil spray or melted **butter**, for greasing
280g **plain flour**
2 tsp **bicarbonate of soda**
¼ tsp **salt**
1 tbsp **ground cinnamon**
1 tsp freshly grated **nutmeg**
2 tsp **ground ginger**
4 large **eggs**
200g **caster sugar**
200g **soft light brown sugar**

250ml **olive oil**
zest of 1 large **orange**, plus extra for decoration
320g **carrots**, grated (about 4 carrots)
150g **currants**

For the cream cheese glaze
150g **full-fat cream cheese**
350g **icing sugar**
2 tbsp **milk**
1 tsp **vanilla bean paste**

These cakes have a pretty shape, which comes from them being baked in mini Bundt tins. Their flavour reminds me of the carrot cakes my mum used to make; although she was never a fan of cakes made with oil, I think for a carrot cake it gives it the perfect texture.

1. Preheat the oven to 180°C (160°C fan oven) mark 4 and grease 12 mini Bundt tins with oil spray or melted butter. Mix the flour, bicarbonate of soda, salt and spices together in a large bowl and set aside.

2. In a medium bowl whisk the eggs, sugars, oil and orange zest together until combined and smooth. Pour onto the flour mixture, add the grated carrots and currants, and mix together well.

3. Fill the Bundt tins about three-quarters full, and bake for 25–30 minutes or until a skewer inserted into the centre of a cake comes out clean and the cake springs back when lightly touched.

4. Allow the cakes to cool in the tins for 10 minutes before turning out onto a wire rack to cool completely. While cooling, make the cream cheese glaze. Put all the ingredients into a bowl and whisk together until smooth. To decorate the cakes, spoon or pipe the glaze onto the cakes and finish with a little grating of orange zest.

TIP

Greasing tins with oil spray is fast and easy, and it covers the tins well. It's especially useful for tins such as Bundt tins. You can now get these sprays at most supermarkets and speciality baking supply shops.

Lemon Tart

SERVES 6–8

	For the filling
150g **plain flour**	finely grated zest of
50g **ground almonds**	4 **lemons**
30g **icing sugar**	125ml **lemon juice**
pinch of **salt**	125g **golden caster sugar**
75g **unsalted butter**, chilled	4 large **eggs**
and diced, plus extra for	150ml **double cream**
greasing	
1 large **egg yolk**	
1 tbsp iced **water**	
½ tsp **vanilla bean paste**	
icing sugar, for dusting	

Lemon tart is one of those classic desserts that hasn't really changed much over time, and that's good because a classic lemon tart is a thing of beauty: fresh, zingy and citrussy – totally delicious. Making this for your mum on Mother's Day will go down a treat – and a what a nice way to say thank you to such a wonderful person.

1. Put the flour, almonds, icing sugar and salt into the bowl of a food processor and pulse to combine. Add the butter and pulse until the mixture resembles coarse breadcrumbs. (Alternatively, rub the butter into the dry ingredients in a large bowl by hand or using a pastry cutter.)

2. Mix the egg yolk, water and vanilla bean paste together and add to the food processor or bowl. Pulse, or mix with a fork, until the dough just starts to come together. Tip onto the work surface and gently knead until the dough comes together into a uniform mass. Press into a flat disc, wrap in clingfilm and chill for 30 minutes.

3. Lightly grease a 23cm fluted tart tin, preferably with a removable base. Roll out the pastry and line the prepared tin. Chill for 15 minutes or until the pastry has firmed up. Preheat the oven to 200°C (180°C fan oven) mark 6.

4. Line the tart shell with baking parchment and fill with a layer of baking beans or rice. Bake for 20 minutes, then remove the baking parchment and baking beans, and bake for a further 5–10 minutes or until the pastry has started to turn golden. Allow the pastry case to cool while you make the filling.

5. Reduce the oven temperature to 160°C (140°C fan oven) mark 2½. Put the lemon zest and juice, sugar and eggs into a medium bowl and whisk gently together until smooth. Pour in the cream and stir gently to combine, without incorporating any air. Pour the filling into the part-baked tart shell and bake for 30 minutes or until the filling has just set. Allow to cool before serving. To serve, dust with a little icing sugar before slicing.

94

Ginger Guinness Cake with Lemon Cream Cheese Frosting

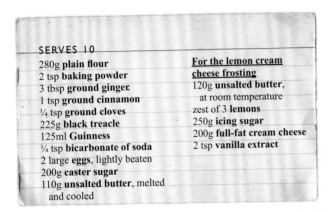

SERVES 10

280g **plain flour**
2 tsp **baking powder**
3 tbsp **ground ginger**
1 tsp **ground cinnamon**
¼ tsp **ground cloves**
225g **black treacle**
125ml **Guinness**
¼ tsp **bicarbonate of soda**
2 large **eggs**, lightly beaten
200g **caster sugar**
110g **unsalted butter**, melted and cooled

For the lemon cream cheese frosting
120g **unsalted butter**, at room temperature
zest of 3 **lemons**
250g **icing sugar**
200g **full-fat cream cheese**
2 tsp **vanilla extract**

Guinness is the sort of drink I always picture dads and granddads drinking, and so this cake seems spot-on for Father's Day. What's more, the good news is that even if you don't like Guinness you will still love the cake, because the main flavour is ginger and the Guinness just helps to give the cake a bit of depth and warmth.

1. Preheat the oven to 180°C (160°C fan oven) mark 4. Grease and line two 23cm cake tins with baking parchment, and grease the baking parchment. Combine the flour, baking powder, ginger, cinnamon and cloves together into a medium bowl and set aside.

2. Put the treacle and Guinness into a medium pan and bring to the boil. Turn off the heat and add the bicarbonate of soda. The mixture will bubble up; set aside until it settles down. In a medium bowl, whisk the eggs and sugar together until thickened and pale. Drizzle in the melted butter and whisk to combine. Whisk the Guinness mixture into the egg mixture.

3. Sift the flour mixture over the liquid ingredients and gently fold together until combined. Divide equally between the prepared tins and bake for 50–60 minutes or until a cocktail stick inserted into the centre of the cakes comes out clean. Allow the cakes to cool in the tins for 15 minutes before turning out onto a wire rack to cool completely.

4. To make the frosting, put the butter and lemon zest into a large bowl and, using an electric mixer, beat until light and smooth, about 5 minutes. Slowly beat in the icing sugar until fully combined, then increase the speed and beat until light and fluffy. Add the cream cheese and vanilla extract, and beat until just combined. Do not over-beat at this stage or the frosting will be too thin.

5. To assemble the cake, put the first cake layer on a cardboard cake board or serving plate and cover the top with a thick layer of frosting. Top with the second layer of cake and spread the remaining frosting on the top of the cake.

Espresso Sablés

MAKES ABOUT 30

160g **unsalted butter**, at room temperature
60g **caster sugar**
60g **light brown sugar**
2 large **egg yolks**
320g **plain flour**, plus extra for dusting
2–3 tsp **finely ground coffee**

For the chocolate ganache filling
110g **dark chocolate** (about 70% cocoa solids), finely chopped
90ml **double cream**
20g **unsalted butter**, softened

When I think of my dad, coffee is one of the things that springs to mind. He has always loved his espresso, but when I was a child I thought it tasted awful even though I loved the smell. Now I love the flavour, and these little sablés taste great and are full of flavour. Serve them with a coffee for the perfect pairing.

1. Put the butter and sugars in the bowl of a food processor and beat until smooth and creamy. Add the egg yolks and pulse until combined. Add the flour and coffee, and pulse until the mixture just starts to come together. (Alternatively, beat the butter and sugars using an electric mixer, then beat in the egg yolks. Add the flour and coffee and gently mix until the mixture just comes together.)

2. Tip the mixture onto the work surface and gently knead together, being careful not to overwork it. Wrap the dough in clingfilm and chill for 30 minutes. Preheat the oven to 180°C (160°C fan oven) mark 4 and line two baking sheets with baking parchment.

3. Roll out the dough on a lightly floured work surface to 2–3mm thick. Using a knife or pizza cutter, cut out about 60 squares of dough about 3cm wide. Put on the baking sheet and bake for 10–12 minutes or until lightly golden, then transfer to a wire rack to cool completely.

4. To make the filling, put the chocolate into a medium heatproof bowl. Put the cream into a small pan over medium heat and bring just to the boil. Pour the cream over the chocolate and leave for a few minutes before gently stirring together to form a silky smooth ganache. Add the butter and mix until combined. Allow to firm up a little, then put into a piping bag with a small plain piping tip and pipe onto the sablés, then sandwich the cookies together.

Chocolate Peanut Butter Cake

SERVES 12

For the peanut dacquoise
40g **egg whites** (about
   1 large egg)
40g **caster sugar**
35g **salted peanuts**,
   finely chopped

For the chocolate cremeux layer
½ sheet **gelatine**
150g **dark chocolate** (about 70%
   cocoa solids), finely chopped

125ml **whole milk**
125g **double cream**
25g **light brown sugar**
2 large **egg yolks**
pinch of **flaked sea salt**

For the caramel filling
75g **granulated sugar**
70ml **double cream**
pinch of **flaked sea salt**
5g **salted butter**, softened

For the peanut butter mousse
2 sheets **gelatine**
250g **smooth peanut butter**
600ml **double cream**
60g **icing sugar**

To finish
200g **double cream**,
   whipped to medium peaks
cocoa powder, for dusting

Peanut butter and chocolate are a well-known and wonderful combination, used here for a rich mousse cake. It's an indulgent dessert to share with lots of people. Although there are several steps, you should find them straightforward to follow, and the recipe uses fairly simple ingredients that are easy to get hold of.

1. To make this dessert you will need a 20cm mousse ring (available from good kitchen suppliers), but if you don't have one and would rather not buy one, you can also use the ring from a 20cm springform cake tin. Put the ring onto a flat plate and set aside. Preheat the oven to 110°C (90°C fan oven) mark ¼ and line a baking sheet with baking parchment.

2. Put the egg whites into a clean, grease-free bowl and whisk until they form soft peaks. With the mixer still on high, slowly pour in the sugar and continue to beat until the meringue holds stiff and glossy peaks.

3. Gently fold in the chopped peanuts. Using an offset spatula, or the back of a spoon, spread the dacquoise mixture onto the prepared baking sheet in a circular shape just over 20cm diameter. Bake for 2 hours or until the meringue is very lightly browned and crisp. Remove from the oven and transfer to a wire rack to cool completely.

4. Press the mousse ring onto the meringue and, using it like a cookie cutter, cut out a disc to fit in the base of the ring. Put the ring and the meringue onto the flat plate and set aside.

5. To make the cremeux layer, put the gelatine into a small bowl and cover with cold water. Put the chocolate into a medium bowl and set aside. Put the milk, cream and half the sugar into a medium pan over medium heat and bring to the boil. While the liquid is heating, whisk the egg yolks with the remaining sugar and the salt.

6. When the milk mixture has just come to the boil, remove it from the heat and pour half over the egg yolks, whisking to combine. Pour the egg mixture into the pan and put back on the heat. Cook, stirring constantly, until the custard coats the back of a spoon. Pour the custard over the chocolate and leave to stand for a few minutes. Add the softened gelatine and stir the mixture together until it is smooth and glossy. Pour the chocolate cremeux into the ring and put in the fridge to set.

7. To make the caramel filling, put the sugar into a medium pan over medium heat and cook until dissolved and dark golden brown in colour, stopping before it starts to smoke. Remove from the heat and carefully pour in half the cream and add the salt. The mixture will bubble violently, so be careful and go slowly.

100

8. Once the mixture has settled, add the remaining cream followed by the butter. If the mixture is lumpy, put it back over low heat and stir until smooth. Pour into a heatproof jug to cool. Pour the cooled caramel filling over the chocolate layer, leaving a 1cm border. Put back into the fridge until needed.

9. To make the peanut butter mousse, put the gelatine into a small bowl and cover with cold water, then set aside for 10 minutes to soften. Put the peanut butter into a small pan and gently warm over low heat so that it becomes more fluid. Add the softened gelatine and whisk to combine.

10. Pour the peanut butter mixture into a large bowl and add the cream and icing sugar, whisking to combine. Chill the mousse mixture for 15–20 minutes, then whisk lightly until the mousse slightly increases in volume. Pour this mousse into the ring and put in the fridge to set.

11. When ready to serve, remove from the fridge and use a blowtorch, or a tea towel soaked in hot water and wrung out, to heat the mousse ring to release it from the dessert. To finish, put the whipped cream into a piping bag fitted with a large plain piping tip and pipe a spiral onto the top of the dessert. Dust the cream with a small amount of cocoa powder.

Chocolate & Guinness Bundt Cake

SERVES 12-16

250g **unsalted butter**, plus
   extra for greasing or an oil spray
200ml **Guinness**
70g **cocoa powder**
350g **plain flour**
1½ tsp **bicarbonate of soda**
½ tsp **salt**
400g **caster sugar**
200ml **soured cream**
3 large **eggs**

For the glaze
100g **dark chocolate**
   (about 70% cocoa solids),
   finely chopped
150ml **double cream**

Suprisingly, chocolate and Guinness are a great combination, and used in a chocolate cake it gives a wonderfully deep flavour. The texture of this cake is quite dense and moist. It's not a light cake for a refined afternoon tea but rather a full-flavoured and comforting cake

1. Preheat the oven to 180°C (160°C fan oven) mark 4 and grease a 1.4l Bundt tin very well – the cake will stick very easily if this pan isn't properly greased; an oil spray is faster and gives a very even coating. Melt the butter in a medium pan. Add the Guinness and cocoa powder, whisking until you have a smooth liquid.

2. In a large bowl, mix together the flour, bicarbonate of soda and salt. Add the sugar, soured cream and eggs to the Guinness mixture and whisk to combine. Pour this over the flour mixture and whisk until you have a smooth batter.

3. Pour the batter into the prepared tin and bake for 40–45 minutes or until the cake springs back when lightly touched; a skewer inserted into the cake will come out with just the odd crumb. Allow to cool in the tin for 15 minutes before turning out onto a wire rack to cool completely. If the cake is domed, use a serrated knife to level it. Turn the cake upside down onto a serving plate.

4. To make the glaze, put the chocolate into a medium heatproof bowl and set aside. Put the cream into a medium pan set over medium heat and bring just to the boil. Pour over the chocolate and allow to stand for a few minutes before stirring gently to form a silky smooth ganache. Allow to cool slightly until it has thickened a little. Pour over the top of the cake, allowing it to drip down the sides.

101

Blackberry & Mint Cake

SERVES 12

225g **unsalted butter** at room temperature, plus extra for greasing
225g **self-raising flour**
2 tsp **baking powder**
225g **caster sugar**
4 large **eggs**, lightly beaten
1–2 tbsp **milk**, if needed
3 tbsp **blackberry** or **blackcurrant liqueur** (optional)
200g **blackberries**

For the mint frosting
175g **unsalted butter** at room temperature
75ml **double cream**
375g **icing sugar**
a pinch of **salt**
¼–½ tsp **peppermint extract**
green food colouring (optional)

For the decoration
100g **dark chocolate** (about 70% cocoa solids), finely chopped
leaves from 1 bunch of **mint**
90g **blackberry jam**
200g **blackberries**

Sometimes you want a decadent triple layer cake, but at other times you want a cake that can be whipped together in no time – and this is one of those cakes. Although it's easy to make, it's still delicious and beautiful to look at.

TIP

To remove the mint leaves easily, the chocolate needs to be fairly thick. If you want to make the decoration easier, just put the leaves onto the cake without peeling them off, the green will look nice and will add another level of flavour.

1. Preheat the oven to 180°C (160°C fan oven) mark 4. Lightly grease and line two 20cm cake tins with baking parchment, greasing the parchment too. In a medium bowl whisk the flour and baking powder together, then set aside.

2. Put the butter and sugar into a large bowl and, using an electric mixer, beat together until light and fluffy, about 5 minutes. Add the eggs, a little at a time, beating until fully combined. With the mixer on low, sift in the flour mixture in three additions mixing until just combined.

3. The cake batter should be a 'dropping consistency', which means that if you take a spoonful of batter out of the bowl it should be soft enough to fall easily from the spoon. If the batter is sticking to the spoon for too long, mix in 1–2 tbsp milk to soften the batter. Add the liqueur and blackberries and gently mix into the batter.

4. Divide the cake batter evenly between the two prepared cake tins and gently level out. Bake for 25–30 minutes or until golden brown and coming away from the edge of the tin; a cocktail stick inserted into the centre of a cake should come out clean. Allow to cool in the tin for 10 minutes before turning out onto a wire rack to cool completely.

5. While the cakes are cooling, make the frosting. Put the butter into a large bowl and, using an electric mixer, beat until light and creamy, about 3 minutes. Slowly incorporate the cream and beat until fully combined. Add the icing sugar, a little at a time, and once fully combined add the salt. Beat on high speed until the frosting is light and fluffy. Add the peppermint extract and colouring, if using, and beat to combine.

6. To make the decoration, melt the chocolate in a heatproof bowl set over a pan of gently simmering water, making sure the base of the bowl doesn't touch the water. Put the mint leaves on a parchment-lined baking sheet. Using a pastry brush, paint one side of each leaf with the melted chocolate. Put the tray in the fridge until the chocolate is set.

7. To assemble the cake, put one of the cake layers on a cardboard cake round or a serving plate. Top with half the frosting and spread evenly across the cake. Top with a thin layer of blackberry jam and then put the second cake layer on top. Spread the remaining buttercream over the top of the cake and sprinkle the blackberries over. Remove the mint leaves from the fridge and carefully peel off the leaves, leaving you with chocolate mint leaves. Put these randomly over the top of the cake.

Mini Ghost Cakes

MAKES 12

115g **unsalted butter** at room
temperature, plus extra for
greasing
175g **plain flour**
2¼ tsp **baking powder**
¼ tsp **salt**
200g **caster sugar**
2 large **eggs**, lightly beaten
1 tsp **vanilla bean paste**
150ml **buttermilk**

For the strawberry frosting
250g **unsalted butter** at
room temperature
2 tsp **vanilla bean paste**
100ml **double cream**
500g **icing sugar**, sifted
a pinch of **salt**
150g sieved **strawberry jam**

For the decoration
720g **white sugarpaste**
icing sugar, for dusting
black edible pen

I know Halloween is about being scary, but these ghost cakes are just too cute to scare anyone. Kids will love them. Why not bake the cakes yourself and then let the kids draw the ghostly faces on the sugarpaste? They'll enjoy letting their imagination run away with them.

1. Preheat the oven to 180°C (160°C fan oven) mark 4 and lightly grease a standard 12-cup muffin pan. In a medium bowl whisk the flour, baking powder and salt together to combine, then set aside.

2. Put the butter and sugar into a large bowl and, using an electric mixer, beat until light and fluffy, about 5 minutes. Add the eggs and vanilla, a little at a time, beating until fully combined.

3. With the mixer on low, add the flour mixture in three additions, alternating with the buttermilk, starting and finishing with the flour. Divide the batter between the prepared cups, filling each about halfway. Bake for 22–25 minutes or until a skewer inserted into the centre of a cake comes out clean.

4. To make the frosting, beat the butter and vanilla paste using an electric mixer until light and creamy. With the mixer on medium speed, slowly incorporate the double cream. Once light and smooth, slowly incorporate the icing sugar and salt, and then beat on high speed until light and fluffy. Add the jam and beat until fully combined.

5. When ready to assemble, use a serrated knife to trim off the tops of the cakes and use the cut side as the base. Top each cake with a mound of frosting, using a small offset spatula to create a smooth domed top.

6. To decorate the cakes, knead the sugarpaste on a work surface lightly dusted with icing sugar until pliable. Divide into 12 balls, each weighing 60g and roll out into circles about 15cm in diameter. Put a circle of sugarpaste onto each cake using your fingers to drape it over the sides of the cake and create pleats around the base. Use an edible pen to draw on ghostly features.

104

Eyeball Cupcakes

MAKES 12

175g **plain flour**	2 tsp **vanilla bean paste**
2¼ tsp **baking powder**	100ml **double cream**
¼ tsp **salt**	500g **icing sugar**
115g **unsalted butter** at room	a pinch of **salt**
temperature	
200g **caster sugar**	**For the decoration**
2 medium **eggs**, lightly beaten	100g **white sugarpaste**
1 tsp **vanilla bean paste**	**black gel food colouring**
150ml **buttermilk**	125g **icing sugar**
	red gel food colouring
For the vanilla buttercream	250g **raspberry** or
250g **unsalted butter** at room	**strawberry jam**
temperature	

These little cakes will add a little drama to your Halloween party. The kids will just love them and would probably enjoy helping to make and decorate them. You could have everything made and ready, and then get a bunch of kids together to hold a mini bake off and see who decorates the best cupcake.

1. Preheat the oven to 180°C (160°C fan oven) mark 4. Line a standard 12-cup muffin pan with paper cases. In a medium bowl, whisk the flour, baking powder and salt together to combine, then set aside.

2. Put the butter and sugar into a large bowl and, using an electric mixer, beat until light and fluffy, about 5 minutes. Add the eggs and vanilla, a little at a time, beating well after each addition.

3. Add the flour mixture in three additions, alternating with the buttermilk, starting and finishing with the flour mixture. Divide the batter between the prepared muffin cups, filling each case about half-full. Bake for 22–25 minutes or until a cocktail stick inserted into the centre comes out clean.

4. To make the buttercream, put the butter and vanilla paste into a large bowl and, using an electric mixer, beat until light and creamy, about 3 minutes. With the mixer on medium speed, slowly pour in the cream, mixing until fully combined. Add the icing sugar and salt, a little at a time, beating until fully combined. Once the sugar is fully incorporated, turn the mixer to high and beat until the buttercream is light and fluffy.

5. For the decorations, divide the sugarpaste into two batches, one slightly larger than the other. Dip a cocktail stick into the black colouring, add to the smaller portion and knead until you have uniform black sugarpaste. Roll both portions of sugarpaste out about 2mm thick. Cut out 12 white discs 2.5cm in diameter and 12 black discs 1cm in diameter. For the red veins, mix the icing sugar together with 1 tbsp water until you have a thick, just pourable mixture. Use a cocktail stick to add a small amount of red colouring and mix to combine.

6. To assemble the cakes, make a small hole in each cake using an apple corer or a sharp knife and fill with a little jam. Spread a layer of buttercream on top of each cake, trying to make it as smooth as possible. Put the red icing into a piping bag fitted with a small piping tip (or put the icing into a freezer bag and cut a small hole in one of the corners). Pipe veins onto the frosting of each cake and then top with the white and black sugarpaste discs, glueing them together with red icing.

Nutty Bone Brownies

MAKES 7

180g **plain flour**
3 tbsp **cocoa powder**
¼ tsp **salt**
300g **dark chocolate** (about 70% cocoa solids), finely chopped
150g **unsalted butter**
4 large **eggs**
150g **caster sugar**
220g **soft light brown sugar**
1 tsp **vanilla extract**
150g **pecans**, finely chopped

Brownies are a firm favourite, because they are simple to make and taste so good! Normally I like mine plain with no nuts and no additions, but this version made with pecans is just wonderful. To make them a bit more seasonal I have used a bone-shaped cookie cutter to make bone-shaped brownies; of course, if you prefer, you can serve these as traditional squares.

1. Preheat the oven to 180°C (160°C fan oven) mark 4. Grease a 23 × 33cm baking tray or brownie pan and line with a strip of baking parchment, leaving a 5cm overhang along the long edges to make removing the brownies easier. In a medium bowl whisk the flour, cocoa powder and salt together to combine, then set aside.

2. Put the butter and chocolate into a medium heatproof bowl set over a pan of gently simmering water, making sure the base of the bowl doesn't touch the water. Heat until fully melted, stirring frequently. Remove from the heat and set aside to cool slightly. Using an electric mixer, whisk the eggs and sugars until thickened and pale – this is called the ribbon stage. Whisk in the cooled chocolate mixture and the vanilla, and then add the flour mixture and pecans. Fold in until just combined – the odd speck of flour showing is fine.

3. Pour the batter into the prepared tin and level out with a spatula. Bake for 25–30 minutes or until a cocktail stick inserted in the centre comes out with just a few moist crumbs. Allow to cool completely in the tin before removing and cutting with a 5cm long bone-shaped cookie cutter, trying to get as many shapes as possible.

TIP

The leftover brownie trimmings can be used to make a delicious ice cream sundae. Mix the brownie bits with ice cream, pecans and some warm chocolate sauce – simple but delicious.

MY NANNA WITH HER SISTERS

Jack-O'-Lantern Cakes

MAKES 4 CAKES (EACH SERVING 2 PEOPLE)

150g **unsalted butter**, melted and cooled, plus extra for greasing
225g **plain flour**
2 tsp **baking powder**
½ tsp **salt**
2 tsp **ground cinnamon**
1 tsp **mixed spice**
¼ tsp **ground cloves**
200g **pumpkin purée** (see Tips)
100ml **plain yogurt**
185g **light brown sugar**

2 large **eggs**
1 tsp **vanilla bean paste**

For the cream cheese frosting

250g **unsalted butter** at room temperature
500g **icing sugar**, sifted
400g **full-fat cream cheese**
1 tsp **vanilla extract**
orange gel colouring
a little **black royal icing**

These little cakes, flavoured with pumpkin, are perfect for a Halloween party. Once decorated they look just like mini Jack-o'-lanterns, and rather adorable they are too. You will need two mini bundlette trays to make the cakes, or you can make a single cake (see Tips).

1. Preheat the oven to 180°C (160°C fan oven) mark 4 and grease eight mini bundlette cups. In a medium bowl, whisk together the flour, baking powder, salt and spices, then set aside.

2. In a large bowl add the pumpkin purée with the yogurt, sugar, eggs, vanilla paste and butter, then mix together until evenly combined. Sift the flour mixture over the liquid ingredients and gently fold together until the dry ingredients are incorporated (don't beat the batter or the cake will be tough).

3. Divide the mixture between the prepared moulds, filling about half-full and bake for 20–25 minutes until the cakes are risen and golden brown, and a skewer inserted into the centre of a cake comes out clean. Allow the cakes to cool in the tin for 10 minutes before turning out onto a wire rack to cool completely.

4. To make the frosting, put the butter into a large bowl and, using an electric mixer, beat until light and smooth, about 3 minutes. Slowly beat in the icing sugar until fully combined, then increase the speed and beat until light and fluffy. Add the cream cheese and vanilla extract, and beat until just combined. Do not over-beat or the frosting will be too thin. Colour the frosting with a very small amount of orange gel colouring and mix to combine.

5. To assemble, use a serrated knife to remove the top of each cake to make it flat. Sandwich two cakes together with a little frosting, and then use a small offset spatula or the back of a spoon to coat the cakes in a layer of frosting. If you like, you can pipe a face on the lanterns using a little black royal icing and a small plain piping tip in the piping bag. To make the stalks for the pumpkins, roll a small amount of green sugarpaste into a thin sausage and cut a short piece for each cake, placing it on the top.

TIP

If you prefer, you can make a single cake using a 450g loaf tin, although it won't have the same pumpkin shape. Bake for 50 minutes at 180°C (160°C fan oven) mark 4.

TIP

You can use canned pumpkin if you can find it or use 200g pumpkin boiled or steamed until tender, then drained and puréed using a blender.

Classic Christmas Cake

SERVES 15-20

225g **sultanas**	225g **plain flour**
225g **raisins**	110g **ground almonds**
225g **currants**	¼ tsp **salt**
110g **mixed peel**	1½ tsp **ground cinnamon**
110g **glacé cherries**	1½ tsp **mixed spice**
zest of 1 **lemon**	225g **caster sugar**
zest of 1 **orange**	5 large **eggs**, lightly beaten
4 tbsp **brandy**	
225g **unsalted butter** at room temperature, plus extra for greasing	

For the almond paste	1 tsp **almond extract**, or to taste
175g **icing sugar**	1 tbsp **rum**
350g **ground almonds**	4 tbsp **apricot jam**, sieved
175g **caster sugar**, plus extra for dusting	
1 large **egg**	**For the icing**
1 large **egg white**	450g **royal icing sugar** or 1.25kg **white sugarpaste**

The smell of a Christmas cake baking means the season has really started. It fills the kitchen and the house with a beautifully warming aroma, which to most people is the smell of Christmas. To decorate the cake you can either use royal icing, which is my preference, or you can cover it with sugarpaste. Either way, if you are making the cake weeks or months in advance, store the cake undecorated and well wrapped in clingfilm, then cover it in almond paste and icing nearer the time.

1. The night before you want to make the cake, put the fruits, zests and brandy into a large bowl and mix together. Cover with clingfilm and leave to soak overnight.

2. Next day, preheat the oven to 150°C (130°C fan oven) mark 2, then grease and triple-line a deep 25.5cm cake tin with baking parchment. In a medium bowl whisk the flour, almonds, salt and spices together to combine, then set aside.

3. Put the butter and sugar into a large bowl and, using an electric mixer, beat until light and fluffy, about 5 minutes. Beat in the eggs, a little at a time, beating until fully combined. With the mixer on low, add the flour mixture, a large spoonful at a time, mixing until just combined. Using a large spatula or metal spoon, fold in the fruit.

4. Scrape the batter into the prepared tin and bake for 1 hour. Reduce the temperature to 110°C (90°C fan oven) mark ¼ and bake for a further 2 hours or until a cocktail stick inserted into the centre comes out clean. If the cake is browning too quickly, put a tent of foil over the top. Allow the cake to cool completely in the tin before removing.

5. To make the almond paste, sift the icing sugar and ground almonds into a large bowl, to break up any lumps. Add the caster sugar and mix to combine. Pour in the egg and egg white, almond extract and rum and, using a wooden spoon, mix to form a stiff dough. Wrap in clingfilm and chill until needed.

6. To assemble the cake, put the apricot jam into a small pan with 1 tbsp water and cook until the jam is bubbling. Brush the cake all over with the jam, which will act as a glue for the almond paste.

7. Divide the almond paste into two portions. Dust the work surface with a little icing sugar and roll the first portion of almond paste into a strip to fit around the cake, but very slightly taller than the cake. Gently press around the outside of the cake, using the palms of your hands to smooth the paste around the cake.

8. Take the second portion of almond paste and roll out into a 25.5cm circle to fit onto the top. Put the paste onto the cake, applying gentle pressure to stick it to the surface. Using the palms of your hands, gently press the edges of the two pieces of almond paste together and smooth them together to eliminate any seal. Allow the cake to dry overnight before icing.

111

9. If using royal icing, put the royal icing sugar into a large bowl with 75ml water. Using a wooden spoon, beat together until it forms a thick and smooth paste. Pour the icing on top of the cake and, using an offset spatula or palette knife, spread the icing across the top and sides of the cake. To finish, you can use the spatula to spike the icing, giving it the look of snow, if you like. If you want a smooth finish, warm the offset spatula in a jug of boiling water, then dry with kitchen paper and use the hot spatula to smooth out the icing.

10. If using sugarpaste, take the white sugarpaste and knead it until pliable. The colder the sugarpaste the longer it will need to be worked with to soften it. Lightly dust the work surface with a little icing sugar and roll out the sugarpaste until it is large enough to cover the cake. The easiest way to do this is to take a piece of string and use it as a guide. Drape it over the cake and grip it where it meets the table. Lift the string from the cake and use this as a measure for your sugarpaste. Brush the almond paste with a little water to make the surface slightly tacky. Using the flats of your hands and arms, drape the sugarpaste over the cake, and use the palms of your hands to smooth the top, applying a gentle pressure. Carefully work your way around the cake, gently smoothing the sugarpaste onto the sides, and trimming off the excess.

11. You can then decorate the cake as you wish. My preference is to wrap the cake in a strip of ribbon and then top with a few shop-bought decorations my family has had for years.

Modern Christmas Cake

SERVES 12

325g **plain flour**
50g **cornflour**
4½ tsp **baking powder**
½ tsp **salt**
225g **unsalted butter** at room temperature, plus extra for greasing
350g **caster sugar**
2 tsp **vanilla extract**
4 medium **eggs**, lightly beaten
240ml **whole milk**

150g **cranberry sauce**
holly leaf decorations (optional)

For the sugared cranberries
100g **caster sugar**, plus extra for coating
1 **cinnamon stick**
50g **cranberries**

For the white chocolate Italian meringue buttercream
150g **white chocolate**, finely chopped
250g caster sugar
6 medium egg whites
450g unsalted butter at room temperature

If you're one of the many people who really dislikes fruit cake, here is something a little different. I have kept the frosting white so that it resembles the more usual Christmas cake, but it is actually flavoured with white chocolate and cranberries. The cake has a real elegance, because it is decorated with sugared cranberries and holly, a perfect centrepiece for the Christmas table.

1. First make the sugared cranberries. Put the sugar into a small pan with 100ml water and bring to the boil. Reduce the temperature to medium and cook the syrup at a simmer for 5 minutes or until the sugar has fully dissolved. Add the cinnamon stick and remove the pan from the heat. Put the cranberries in a container with a tight-fitting lid and, once the syrup has cooled slightly, pour it over the cranberries and seal the container. Cool, then pop in the fridge overnight.

2. Remove the cranberries from the fridge and drain thoroughly. Roll them in caster sugar and set aside to dry for 2 hours. Preheat the oven to 180°C (160°C fan oven) mark 4, then grease and line three 20cm cake tins with baking parchment, greasing the parchment too.

112

3. In a medium bowl whisk the flour, cornflour, baking powder and salt together to combine, then set aside. Put the butter into a large bowl and, using an electric mixer, beat on medium–high speed until smooth and light. Add the sugar and beat until light and fluffy, about 5 minutes. Add the vanilla and mix to combine. With the mixer on medium speed, add the eggs, a little at a time, beating until fully combined before adding more. With the mixer on low, sift in the flour mixture alternating with the milk, in three additions starting and finishing with the flour.

4. Divide the batter evenly among the prepared tins and bake for 30–35 minutes or until the cakes are golden brown and spring back when lightly touched. Allow the cakes to cool in the tins for 10 minutes before turning out onto a wire rack to cool completely.

5. To make the buttercream, melt the white chocolate in a heatproof bowl set over a pan of gently simmering water, making sure the base of the bowl doesn't touch the water. Remove from the heat and allow to cool.

6. Put 160ml water and the sugar into a pan over medium heat, and have a sugar thermometer ready. Put the egg whites into a clean, grease-free bowl (this is best done using a freestanding electric mixer). As the syrup reaches about 115°C, start whisking on high speed. Cook until the syrup registers 121°C, then remove from the heat and, with the mixer still running, pour the syrup in a slow stream down the side of the bowl containing the whites, avoiding the beaters. Continue whisking on high speed until the meringue is at room temperature.

7. With the mixer on medium–high speed, add the butter, a few pieces at a time, beating until fully combined. When adding the butter it can sometimes look curdled, if this happens, don't worry, just keep mixing and eventually it will smooth out again forming a light buttercream. Pour in the melted and cooled white chocolate and mix to combine fully.

8. To assemble the cake, put the first cake layer on a cardboard cake round or a serving plate and top with a layer of the buttercream. Spread half the cranberry sauce on top, leaving a 2cm border. Top with the second cake layer and repeat as before, then top with the last layer of cake. Spread the remaining buttercream across the top and sides of the cake. Top with the sugared cranberries and some holly leaves.

Coconut & Raspberry Cake

SERVES 12	
225g **unsalted butter** at room temperature, plus extra for greasing	**For the coconut crème mousseline**
325g **plain flour**	5 large **egg yolks**
50g **cornflour**	200g **caster sugar**
4½ tsp **baking powder**	50g **plain flour**
½ tsp **salt**	400ml **coconut milk**
400g **caster sugar**	100ml **whole milk**
2 tsp **vanilla extract**	450g **unsalted butter** at room temperature
5 medium **egg whites**	1 tsp **vanilla bean paste**
150ml **whole milk**	2 tsp **coconut extract**, or to taste
150ml **coconut milk**	
	To finish
	200g **raspberry jam**
	250g **sweetened desiccated coconut**

I know coconut comes across as tropical, summery even, but a cake that's covered in coconut just looks really Christmassy to me – it looks like freshly fallen snow. The frosting for this cake is very different from regular buttercream or frostings. It has a base of thickened coconut custard, to which you add butter, and this forms a beautifully light crème mousseline. Because the crème isn't very sweet, my preference is to cover the cake with sweetened desiccated coconut, but if you prefer, you can, of course, just use unsweetened.

1. To make the mousseline, in a large bowl whisk the egg yolks, sugar and flour together to form a thick paste. Put the coconut milk and whole milk into a large pan over medium–high heat and bring to the boil. Remove from the heat and pour half the milk mixture into the egg mixture, whisking to combine.

2. Pour the egg mixture into the pan and whisk to combine. Put the pan back on the heat and whisk continuously until the mixture boils, then whisk for a further 3 minutes – the custard should be very thick.

3. Pour the thickened custard back into the bowl and allow it to cool for a few minutes. Add the softened butter, vanilla bean paste and coconut extract. Whisk to combine, then press some clingfilm to the surface and chill for 50–60 minutes or until the mousseline has the texture of buttercream.

4. Preheat the oven to 180°C (160°C fan oven) mark 4, then grease and line three 20cm cake tins with baking parchment, and grease the baking parchment. In a medium bowl whisk the flour, cornflour, baking powder and salt together to combine, then set aside. Put the butter into a large bowl and, using an electric mixer, beat on medium–high speed until smooth and light about 3 minutes. Add the sugar and beat until light and fluffy, about 5 minutes. Add the vanilla and mix to combine. With the mixer on medium, add the egg whites, a little at a time, beating until fully combined before adding more. Mix together the milk and coconut milk. With the mixer on low, add the flour mixture to the butter mixture in three additions, alternating with the milks, and starting and finishing with the flour.

5. Divide the batter evenly among the prepared tins and bake for 30–35 minutes or until the cakes spring back when lightly touched. Allow the cakes to cool in the tins for 10 minutes before turning out onto a wire rack to cool completely.

6. To assemble the cake, put the first cake layer onto a cardboard cake round or a serving plate and top with a layer of the crème mousseline. Spread half the jam over the mousseline and top with a second layer of cake. Repeat the process. Spread the remaining mousseline over the top and sides of the cake, then coat the whole cake in the desiccated coconut.

114

Black Forest Roulade

SERVES 8

butter, for greasing
60g **plain flour**, plus extra
  for dusting
4 large **eggs**
100g **caster sugar**
40g **cocoa powder**, plus extra
  for dusting
25g **unsalted butter**, melted
  and cooled

For the filling
175g **cherries**, pitted and
  halved
about 3 tbsp **kirsch**
300ml **double cream**
150g **cherry jam**

For the ganache topping
100ml **double cream**
100g **dark chocolate** (about
  70% cocoa solids), finely
  chopped

Ever since I have known my boyfriend I have made him whatever cake he wants for his birthday. This past year he asked for something with the classic Black Forest flavours of chocolate, cherries and cream. As we wanted something fast to make, this roulade was perfect, as it can be whipped up in no time – it will probably be gone in no time too, just what you need during a busy festive period.

1. Preheat the oven to 180°C (160°C fan oven) mark 4, then grease and line a 27 × 39cm high-sided baking tray or brownie pan with baking parchment. Grease the baking parchment and dust with flour, tapping out any excess. Put the eggs and sugar in a heatproof bowl set over a pan of gently simmering water, making sure the base of the bowl doesn't touch the water. Whisk constantly until the sugar has dissolved and the mixture is just warm to the touch.

2. Remove the bowl from the pan and, using an electric mixer, whisk for 5 minutes on high speed, then reduce the speed to medium and whisk for a further 3 minutes. By this stage the mixture should have tripled in volume, and when the whisk is lifted from the bowl it should form a slowly dissolving ribbon.

3. Sift in the flour and cocoa and gently fold together, making sure that all the dry ingredients are combined but trying to keep as much volume as possible. Take a large spoonful of the batter and add it to the melted butter, then mix together (this will lighten the butter and help to incorporate it into the batter). Gently fold this into the batter.

4. Pour the batter into the prepared tray and very gently level out. Bake for 15 minutes or until the cake has risen; a skewer inserted into the centre should come out clean. Allow to cool in the tray for 10 minutes before turning out onto a wire rack to cool completely.

5. While the cake is baking, make the filling. Put the cherries into a small bowl, pour over 3 tbsp kirsch and allow to macerate.

6. When ready to assemble, whisk the cream until it holds medium-firm peaks. Drain the cherries from the kirsch and use the liquid to brush across the cake, adding a little extra kirsch if needed. Brush the cake with a thin layer of cherry jam, and then spread the cream evenly over the cake. Scatter the cherries across the cream.

7. Carefully roll the cake into a log, along the short edge, and place onto a serving plate. To finish the cake, put the cream for the ganache into a small pan over medium heat and just bring to the boil. Put the chocolate into a medium heatproof bowl and pour the hot cream over. Allow to stand for a few minutes before stirring gently to form a silky smooth ganache. Leave to stand for a while until it has thickened. Spread the ganache all over the roulade and dust with a little cocoa powder to finish.

Stollen

MAKES 1 LARGE LOAF

250ml **whole milk**
100g **unsalted butter**
500g **strong bread flour**,
   plus extra for dusting
1 tsp **mixed spice**
50g **caster sugar**
1 tsp **salt**
7g **fast-action yeast**
1 large **egg**
zest of 1 large **lemon**
150g **mixed dried fruit**

25g **mixed candied peel**
25g **almonds**, roughly
   chopped
oil, for greasing
200g **marzipan**
50g **unsalted butter**, melted
icing sugar, for dusting

Many countries across the world have unique baking traditions at Christmastime. The British have Christmas cake and figgy pudding, and the Germans have stollen, a sweet, fruity bread dough with marzipan running through the centre. Although not difficult to make, stollen does take a little effort, and as such I think it makes a brilliant gift during the festive period.

1. Line a baking sheet with baking parchment. Put the milk and butter into a small pan over low heat and heat until the butter has melted. Allow the mixture to stand until it is just lukewarm.

2. In a large bowl, mix the flour, mixed spice, sugar, salt and yeast together. Add the milk mixture and the egg, and mix together with a wooden spoon or your hands to form a soft dough. Lightly flour the work surface and tip the dough onto it. Knead the dough for 10 minutes or until smooth and elastic.

3. Flatten the dough and sprinkle over the lemon zest, dried fruit, candied peel and chopped almonds, and knead to distribute evenly. Put the dough in a lightly oiled bowl and cover with clingfilm. Put the bowl into a warm place and leave to rise for 1 hour or until doubled in size.

4. Tip the dough onto the floured work surface and lightly knead to knock out some of the air. Press or roll into a 25 × 35cm rectangle. Roll the marzipan into a 25cm long log and put it into the centre of the dough. Lightly brush the edges of the dough with water and fold the dough over the marzipan, then press together to seal. Put the stollen onto the prepared baking sheet. Lightly cover with clingfilm and leave to rise for 30 minutes or until doubled in size. Meanwhile, preheat the oven to 190°C (170°C fan oven) mark 5.

5. Brush the stollen all over with half the melted butter. Bake for 35–40 minutes or until browned and the stollen sounds hollow when tapped underneath. Transfer to a wire rack to cool for 5 minutes, then brush the loaf with the remaining melted butter and dust with icing sugar. Leave to cool.

Buche de Noel

SERVES 10

For the chocolate mousse
250g good-quality **milk chocolate**, finely chopped
600ml **double cream**

For the hazelnut dacquoise base
75g **egg whites** (about 1½ large eggs)
75g **caster sugar**
70g finely chopped **hazelnuts**
a pinch of **salt**

For the chocolate crunch layer
100g good-quality **milk chocolate**
275g **Nutella**
50g **crisped rice cereal**

For the caramelised pear filling
15g **unsalted butter** .
15g **light brown sugar**
2 large **Conference pears**, peeled, cored and diced

For the glaze
125g **dark chocolate** (about 70% cocoa solids), finely chopped
225ml **double cream**
3 tbsp **golden syrup**

hazelnuts and **edible gold powder**, to decorate

I know this recipe has many steps and a long list of ingredients, but I do hope you will give it a go, because all the stages are fairly easy, it just takes time to construct. Imagine how happy your guests will be when you present them with this amazing Parisian-style buche de noel, or yule log, as we would call it. To make this dessert you will need a 26 x 8 x 7.5cm stainless steel U-shaped terrine mould (also called a buche de noel mould). Alternatively, you could make this in a standard 23 x 10cm loaf tin, but the cake won't have the same shape. You also need time, so make this on a day that you can dedicate to baking.

1. For the chocolate mousse, melt 165g of the milk chocolate in a heatproof bowl set over a pan of gently simmering water, making sure the base of the bowl doesn't touch the water. Remove from the heat and allow to cool. Pour 400ml of the double cream into a large bowl and whisk until the mixture barely holds soft peaks.

2. Pour the cooled melted chocolate into the cream and whisk until the mixture is light but holds stiff peaks. Fill a 26 × 8 × 7.5cm stainless steel U-shaped terrine mould with this mousse mixture, levelling it evenly. Use the rounded tip of a palette knife to make a U-shaped depression along the centre of the mould. (This will be filled with pear later.) Wrap the mould in clingfilm and freeze for 3 hours or until firm.

3. To make the dacquoise, preheat the oven to 110°C (90°C fan oven) mark ¼ and line a baking sheet with baking parchment. Put the egg whites into a clean, grease-free bowl and, using an electric mixer, whisk until they form soft peaks. With the mixer still on high, slowly pour in the sugar and continue to beat until the meringue holds stiff and glossy peaks.

4. Gently fold in the chopped hazelnuts and salt. Using an offset spatula or the back of a spoon, spread the dacquoise mixture onto the prepared baking sheet in a rectangular shape just bigger than the terrine mould. Bake for 2 hours or until the meringue is very lightly browned and crisp. Remove from the oven and transfer to a wire rack to cool completely.

5. To make the chocolate crunch layer, melt the chocolate and Nutella in the microwave or in a heatproof bowl set over a pan of gently simmering water. Remove from the heat and allow to cool slightly, then add the crisped rice cereal and mix to combine. Spread this mixture in an even layer over the cooled dacquoise.

6. To make the pear filling, melt the butter in a medium frying pan over medium heat and add the sugar. Cook for a few minutes until the mixture is bubbling. Add the diced pears and cook, stirring occasionally, for 3–5 minutes or until the pears are caramelised and slightly softened. Tip the pears and any remaining caramel into a small bowl, then cover and set aside until needed. (You can make the pear mixture a day ahead, then cover it with clingfilm and chill, if you like.)

121

7. Remove the mould from the freezer and take off the clingfilm. Fill the U-shaped depression with the caramelised pears, trying to add as little caramel as possible. Make another batch of mousse with the remaining ingredients and cover the pear with this batch. Leave a small amount of space in the mould for the final layers.

8. Turn the mould onto the dacquoise and crunch layers. Firmly press the mould down onto the dacquoise, using the mould edges like a cookie cutter. Remove the excess mixture from around the outside of the mould and then wrap the mould in clingfilm and freeze for at least another 3 hours.

9. Remove the mould from the freezer and invert it onto a wire rack set over a rimmed baking tray. Using a blowtorch, or a very hot cloth, heat the outside of the mould to release the buche. To make the glaze, melt the chocolate, cream and golden syrup in a small pan over low heat. Once smooth and shiny, remove from the heat and allow to cool slightly.

10. To finish the buche, pour the glaze evenly over the mousse, making sure to cover the sides as well as the top. Using a large offset spatula, gently move the buche off the wire rack and onto a serving plate, then transfer to the fridge for a few hours before serving; this will allow the mousse to soften and all the textures to be perfect for eating. (Once fully assembled, the buche will keep well in the fridge for two days.) To decorate, cover a few hazelnuts in edible gold powder and scatter across the top of the dessert.

Figgy Pudding

SERVES 6

100g **raisins**	115g **unsalted butter** at room temperature, plus extra for greasing
10g **currants**	
100g **sultanas**	1½ tbsp **black treacle**
60g **dried figs**	2 large **eggs**
60g **dried dates**	150g **self-raising flour**
1 small eating **apple**, peeled and grated	1 tsp **mixed spice**
60ml **rum** or **brandy**	½ tsp **ground cinnamon**
115g **light brown sugar**	¼ tsp freshly grated **nutmeg**

In the Christmas song 'We wish You a Merry Christmas' most kids enjoy it when they get to the line where they demand to be brought some figgy pudding – the classic Christmas dish. My version is lighter than the usual normal Christmas pudding, it isn't stodgy but it still has a boozy flavour. This version is very easy to make and, as it isn't a traditional one, I wouldn't recommend storing for months, it really is best served within a couple days of making.

1. The night before you want to make the pudding, put the raisins, currants and sultanas into a medium bowl. Chop the figs and dates so that they are roughly the same size as the rest of the dried fruit. Add to the bowl with the grated apple. Pour over the rum or brandy and mix to combine. Cover the bowl with clingfilm and set aside overnight to soak.

2. The next day, put the sugar, butter and treacle into a medium bowl and beat together until light and fluffy, about 5 minutes. Add the eggs, one at a time, beating until fully combined before adding the next. Sift the flour and spices over the butter mixture and fold to combine. Add the fruit and stir until evenly combined.

3. Grease a 1 litre pudding bowl with softened butter, and then scrape the batter into the bowl, pressing it in firmly. Cut a large piece of foil and make a fold in the middle to create a pleat. Cover the basin with the foil and secure by tying a piece of kitchen string around the bowl.

4. Put a small plate upside down in a large pan and put the bowl on top. Fill the pan with enough water to come halfway up the pudding basin, then cover with a lid. Place over high heat and bring the water to the boil. Reduce the temperature so that the water is at a gentle simmer, and cook the pudding for 2 hours. Remove the pan from the heat and carefully remove the pudding. To serve, unwrap and invert onto a serving plate.

MATTY STARTING YOUNG

Christmas Tree Decoration Cookies

MAKES 25

425g **plain flour**, plus extra
for dusting
½ tsp **salt**
200g **caster sugar**
1 tsp **mixed spice**
½ tsp **ground cinnamon**
¼ tsp freshly grated **nutmeg**
225g **unsalted butter**
1 large **egg**
1 large **egg yolk**
1 tsp **vanilla bean paste**

**For the royal icing
decoration**
450g **royal icing sugar**
gel food colourings
(optional)

There is something very satisfying about making the decorations for your own Christmas tree or even making a batch of these cookies as a gift for friends or family. If you want the cookies to last longer, you can also make them with the dough for my Gingerbread House on page 128.

1. Line two baking sheets with baking parchment. Put the flour, salt, sugar and spices in the bowl of a food processor and pulse to combine. Add the butter and pulse until the mixture resembles coarse breadcrumbs. (Alternatively, mix the dry ingredients in a large bowl and rub the butter into the flour by hand or using a pastry cutter.)

2. Add the egg, yolk and vanilla paste and pulse (or stir) until the mixture just comes together. Tip onto a lightly floured work surface and gently knead together until uniform. Divide the dough in half and wrap in clingfilm, then chill for about 1 hour.

3. Working with one half of the dough at a time, roll out to a thickness of 5mm. Cut out as many shapes as possible using Christmas cookie cutters. Re-roll the scraps to cut out more cookies. Lift the cookies off the surface with a spatula and place onto the prepared baking sheets. Chill for 15–20 minutes. Preheat the oven to 180°C (160°C fan oven) mark 4.

4. Use a skewer to press a hole into the cookies – this will be used to thread the ribbon to hang the cookies. Bake the cookies for 13–15 minutes or until the edges turn golden. Allow to cool on the baking sheets for 10 minutes before transferring to a wire rack to cool completely.

5. To make the royal icing, put the royal icing sugar in a large bowl with 70ml water and mix together until you have a thick, barely pourable, paste. Divide the icing between two bowls and add 1–2 tsp water to one bowl, then mix well. This icing should be slightly thinner than the first mixture.

6. Depending on how many styles of cookie you want to make, you can divide the icings into smaller batches to colour them as you wish. To add the colour, use a cocktail stick to add just a little, then stir to combine evenly. To decorate the cookies, put the thicker icing into a piping bag fitted with a thin (no. 2) piping tube. Pipe around the outside of the cookies; this will act as a barrier to prevent the icing running off the edges. Make sure to pipe around the hole for the ribbon as well. Allow this to set for a few minutes.

7. Put the slightly runnier icing into a piping bag fitted with a slightly wider piping tube (no. 4) and fill the cookie with the icing. You don't need to pipe a layer over the whole cookie, just give it a rough coating and then use a cocktail stick to level out the icing and encourage it into any corners. To get a very clean finish, gently shake the cookie – this will remove any cocktail-stick marks. Allow the icing to set overnight. Insert a thin ribbon through the hole and tie it into a loop. The cookies can now be hung onto the Christmas tree.

124

Snickerdoodles

MAKES 24	
350g **plain flour**	**For the coating**
2 tsp **baking powder**	50g **caster sugar**
1 tsp **salt**	3 tsp **ground cinnamon**
225g **unsalted butter** at room temperature	
200g **caster sugar**	
100g **light brown sugar**	
2 large **eggs**	
1 tsp **vanilla extract**	

For years, I thought snickerdoodles had something to do with the chocolate bar and was expecting something with chocolate, peanuts and caramel, but these classic American cookies are a lot simpler than that. A delicious buttery cookie, crisp on the outside and soft on the inside rolled in cinnamon sugar – absolutely wonderful!

1. Preheat the oven to 180°C (160°C fan oven) mark 4 and line two baking sheets with baking parchment. In a medium bowl whisk the flour, baking powder and salt together to combine, then set aside. To make the coating, in a small bowl mix the sugar and cinnamon together.

2. Put the butter and sugars into a large bowl and, using an electric mixer, beat together until light and fluffy, about 5 minutes. Add the eggs and vanilla, a little at time, beating until fully combined. Add the flour mixture in three additions, beating until just combined.

3. Using a cookie or ice-cream scoop, divide the dough in half. Take one half of the dough and divide it into 12 equal-sized balls (each ball should weigh about 40g – a large tablespoonful of dough). Roll the cookies in the cinnamon sugar and put six on each baking sheet about 5cm apart.

4. Bake for 10–12 minutes or until golden around the edges but still soft in the middle. Allow to cool on the baking sheets for a few minutes before transferring to a wire rack to cool completely. Repeat with the remaining cookie dough.

CHEEKY MONKEYS HELEN AND GEORGE

Lebkuchen

MAKES 24

150ml **clear honey**
150ml **black treacle**
200g **soft dark brown sugar**
2 large **eggs**
500g **plain flour**
2 tsp **baking powder**
1 tsp **bicarbonate of soda**
1 tbsp **ground ginger**
2 tsp **mixed spice**
1 tsp **ground cinnamon**

½ tsp freshly grated **nutmeg**
¼ tsp **ground cloves**
a large pinch of freshly
 ground **black pepper**

For the glaze
100g **icing sugar**
juice of 1 **lemon**

I have to admit that I love the lebkuchen you can buy in foil bags at the supermarket at Christmastime – they are delightfully chewy and spicy. Making a homemade version is actually really easy, so much so that I won't be buying them anymore.

1. Put the honey, black treacle and sugar into a medium pan over medium heat. Stir until the mixture is liquid and the sugar has dissolved. Remove from the heat and allow to cool slightly. Add the eggs and mix to combine. Put all the dry ingredients into a large bowl and whisk together. Pour over the liquid ingredients and mix together until you have a stiff dough. Cover the bowl with clingfilm and chill for 4 hours or until firm.

2. Preheat the oven to 180°C (160°C fan oven) mark 4 and line two baking sheets with baking parchment. Form the dough into 24 tablespoon-sized balls and put 12 balls onto each tray. Flatten each cookie slightly and bake for 10 minutes or until set and lightly browned around the outside. Put the cookies onto a wire rack to cool slightly.

3. To make the glaze, mix the icing sugar and lemon juice in a small bowl until smooth (the mixture should be thin and pourable). While the cookies are still slightly warm, dip them into the glaze, allowing any excess to drip off. Allow the glaze to dry before serving.

TIP

As with all gingerbread recipes, these cookies taste better after a day or two.

127

Gingerbread House

MAKES 1 HOUSE

200g **unsalted butter**
200g **soft dark brown sugar**
4 tbsp **golden syrup**
500g **self-raising flour**, plus extra for dusting
1 tbsp **ground ginger**
2 tsp **mixed spice**
1 tsp **ground cinnamon**
½ tsp freshly grated **nutmeg**

For the decoration

450g **royal icing sugar**
a selection of small **sweets**
desiccated coconut

Making a gingerbread house is such a fun thing to do with kids (or without, if you're a big kid like me), and making them fills the house with a wonderful Christmassy smell of ginger and spices. I have provided a template for a house (see page 166) but you could always make your own and go wild with the decoration.

1. Preheat the oven to 180°C (160°C fan oven) mark 4 and line two baking sheets with baking parchment. In a large pan over medium heat, melt the butter, sugar and golden syrup together. Meanwhile, sift the remaining ingredients together in a medium bowl. Remove the pan from the heat and pour the butter mixture over the dry ingredients, then mix together using a wooden spoon to form a stiff dough.

2. Lightly dust the work surface with flour and roll out the dough until it is 4–5mm thick. Using the house template (see page 166), cut out the house pieces and gently transfer to the prepared baking sheets. Bake for 15–20 minutes or until set around the edges and lightly browned. Cool on the baking sheets for 10 minutes, then transfer to wire racks to cool completely before using to build your house.

3. To assemble the house you will need a board, such as a round or square cardboard cake drum, but you could also use a flat plate or even a cake stand. To make the royal icing, which will act as glue, put the royal icing sugar into a large bowl and add 75ml water. Using a wooden spoon, beat together to form a thick paste. Put the royal icing into a piping bag fitted with a medium plain piping tip. Pipe strips of royal icing onto the edges of the gingerbread pieces.

4. One by one, stick the wall pieces together. To support the house while you build it, put cans next to each wall. Leave the royal icing to dry for at least 1 hour before you attach the roof to the house. Add the roof pieces, supporting the roof edges with cans or books to stop the pieces sliding off while the icing dries.

5. To decorate, use the remaining royal icing to pipe tiles on the roof and to fix sweets all over the house to make your very own Hansel and Gretel-style house. To finish, cover the board in desiccated coconut, to make a snowy scene.

129

afternoon
tea & picnics

Mini Cinnamon & Apple Cakes

MAKES 24 CAKES

110g **unsalted butter**, melted and cooled, plus extra butter for greasing
150g **plain flour**
20g **cornflour**
1½ tsp **baking powder**
2 tsp **ground cinnamon**
1 tsp freshly grated **nutmeg**
¼ tsp **salt**
2 large **eggs**
225g **light brown sugar**

100ml **whole milk**
2 tsp **vanilla extract**

For the topping
6 large eating **apples**, preferably Braeburn
juice of 1 **lemon**
100g **unsalted butter**

For the filling
200ml **double cream**
100g **light brown sugar**

Sometimes you fancy eating a little cake but want something a bit fresher and less sweet than a cupcake. These small spicy cakes fit the bill perfectly. They are filled with a little whipped cream and then topped with some delicious caramelised apples – perfect for a lovely afternoon tea with friends.

1. Preheat the oven to 180°C (160°C fan oven) mark 4 and lightly grease two standard 12-cup muffin pans. In a medium bowl whisk the flour, cornflour, baking powder, cinnamon, nutmeg and salt together to combine, then set aside.

2. Put the eggs and sugar into a large bowl and whisk together until pale and thickened. Pour in the melted butter and whisk to combine. Add the flour mixture in three additions, alternating with the milk and vanilla, starting and finishing with the flour.

3. Divide the batter among the muffin cups and bake for 12–14 minutes or until a cocktail stick inserted into the centre of a cake comes out clean. Allow the cakes to cool in the pan for 10 minutes before transferring to a wire rack to cool completely.

4. To make the topping, peel, core and dice the apples, then toss them in the lemon juice to prevent them browning. Put the butter into a medium pan and melt over medium heat, then add the sugar and leave to dissolve and bubble. Add the apples and cook for a few minutes until slightly softened. Remove from the heat and set aside while you make the filling.

5. Put the cream into a medium bowl and whisk until it holds soft peaks. Make a small hole in the top of each cake using an apple corer or a sharp knife and fill with cream. Top each cake with a small pile of the caramelised apples.

133

Battenburg Cake

MAKES 2 CAKES SERVING 10 EACH

4 large **eggs**
½ tsp **vanilla extract**
¾ tsp **almond extract**·
275g **caster sugar**
185g **unsalted butter**, softened
235g **plain flour**
1 tsp **baking powder**
red and **yellow food colouring**
icing sugar, to dust
500g **marzipan**
170g **raspberry jam**, to fill

This recipe comes from a pastry chef friend of mine called Tim Fisher, and to my mind it tastes exactly like the original cake I remember eating as a child. The version here is the classic: an almond-flavoured cake with raspberry jam filling. One of the reasons I wanted to include this recipe is that it is a great example of the 'high ratio' method, where instead of creaming the butter and sugar you cream the butter with the flour. The result is a cake with a very fine crumb, but one that also stays moist for longer than usual.

1. Preheat the oven to 180°C (160°C fan oven) mark 4 and lightly grease a 23 × 33cm high-sided baking tray or brownie pan. Take a piece of baking parchment a little longer than the tin and make a horizontal fold across the middle the same height as the tin. Use this to line the brownie tin creating a divide in the centre of the tin to stop the two mixtures running into each other.

2. Put the eggs, vanilla extract and almond extract into a large bowl with 70g of the sugar. Using an electric whisk on high speed, whisk the eggs until pale and thick. Gradually whisk in the remaining sugar, and continue to whisk until the eggs are very thick; when the whisk is lifted from the bowl the mixture should form a very thick, slowly dissolving ribbon. Set aside while you prepare the second mixture.

3. Put the butter into a large bowl and sift in the flour and baking powder. Using an electric mixer, cream until light and smooth (it should look a little like cake batter). If your butter isn't soft enough, it will at first look like crumble mixture, but continue beating and eventually the butter and flour will incorporate fully and you will have a smooth batter. Add a quarter of the egg mixture and mix to combine. Repeat with the remaining egg mixture in three additions.

4. Divide the mixture equally between two bowls; this is best done by weight. Add a very small amount of red colouring to one bowl and yellow to the other. Pour the yellow batter into one half of the prepared tin and level it out evenly. Repeat with the pink batter in the second half. Bake for 18–22 minutes or until risen and a cocktail stick inserted into the centre of the cake comes out clean. Allow the cakes to cool in the tin for 15 minutes before turning out onto a wire rack to cool completely.

5. Trim the edges off the cakes and cut each cake lengthways into four equal-sized pieces about 3.5cm wide. To assemble the cakes, divide the marzipan into two pieces. Dust the work surface with icing sugar and roll out each piece into a 16 × 28cm rectangle or large enough to wrap around a completed cake.

6. Brush the marzipan with a thin layer of raspberry jam and put one yellow and one pink piece of cake onto a piece of baking parchment, sticking the touching sides together with more jam.

7. Lift the cake onto the marzipan and wrap with the marzipan, trimming off any excess. Trim both ends of the cake, to give the Battenberg a neat appearance. Repeat to make a second cake.

TIP

The cake, without the jam or marzipan, freezes very well, so you could make one for eating now and freeze one for another time. Freeze for up to 1 month, wrapped very well with clingfilm. Thaw in the fridge and then complete as above.

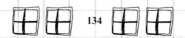

134

Banana Bread

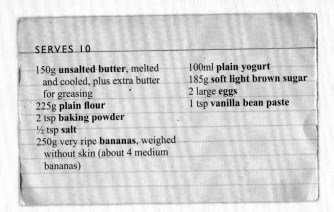

SERVES 10

150g **unsalted butter**, melted and cooled, plus extra butter for greasing
225g **plain flour**
2 tsp **baking powder**
½ tsp **salt**
250g very ripe **bananas**, weighed without skin (about 4 medium bananas)

100ml **plain yogurt**
185g **soft light brown sugar**
2 large **eggs**
1 tsp **vanilla bean paste**

The smell of a banana loaf baking is enough to make me feel all warm and cosy – banana bread is for me the ultimate comfort food. If it isn't eaten immediately, one of my favourite ways to enjoy it is sliced and toasted, then spread with a little salted butter. It's so delicious that you might find yourself eating it that way all the time.

1. Preheat the oven to 180°C (160°C fan oven) mark 4, and grease and line a 450g loaf tin with baking parchment. In a medium bowl, mix the flour, baking powder and salt together. In a large bowl, mash the bananas with the back of a fork until no large lumps remain.

2. Add the yogurt, sugar, eggs, vanilla paste and melted butter, then mix together until evenly combined. Sift the flour mixture over the yogurt mixture and gently fold together until the dry ingredients are incorporated (don't beat the mixture or the cake will be tough).

3. Pour the mixture into the prepared tin and bake for 1 hour or until risen and golden brown. Allow to cool in the tin for 10 minutes before turning out onto a wire rack to cool completely.

TIP

Use very, very ripe bananas – the blacker the better. This way you get that real banana flavour.

Classic Cream Tea

MAKES 10-12

340g **plain flour**, plus extra
for dusting
25g **baking powder** ·
½ tsp **salt**
50g **unsalted butter**, diced
80g **caster sugar**
100ml **whole milk**
3 large **eggs**
60g **sultanas**
clotted cream, to serve

For the quick raspberry jam
400g **raspberries**
400g **caster sugar**

I grew up visiting Devon a lot as a child, and I was always a big fan of the classic cream tea. Throughout the year my mum would often make scones and they were one of the first things I learned to bake. It was also rare that my mum bought raspberry jam. We always had raspberries in the freezer, and whenever we needed some jam either for scones or a trifle, my mum would whip up a batch of her quick raspberry jam. Really, there is little that beats a fresh scone with homemade jam and lashings of clotted cream.

1. To make the raspberry jam, put the raspberries into a large pan and cook for a few minutes over medium–low heat until the fruit begins to release its juice. Stir in the sugar, then cook for a few minutes until the sugar has dissolved. Increase the heat and boil for 10 minutes. Pour the jam into two sterilised jars and seal. Cool and store in the fridge until needed.

2. Line a baking sheet with baking parchment. In a medium bowl whisk the flour, baking powder and salt together to combine. Add the diced butter and rub into the flour until it resembles fine breadcrumbs. Mix in the sugar, then add the milk, 2 of the eggs and the sultanas. Using a wooden spoon, mix the ingredients until they just come together and form a soft wet dough.

3. Tip the dough out onto a well floured work surface and gently knead by folding the dough in half and then turning it 45 degrees and repeating until the dough is smooth. Be careful not to over-knead the dough – it only needs a very brief, light touch, you're not kneading bread.

4. Lightly flour the surface of the dough and roll out to about 2.5cm thick. Using a 7cm plain round cutter, cut out as many scones as you can. Don't twist the cutter when forming the scones but use a firm downwards press, this will help the scones to rise properly. Make more scones with the trimmings. Put the scones on the baking sheet and allow to rest for 1 hour before baking.

5. Preheat the oven to 200°C (180°C fan oven) mark 6. Make an egg wash by mixing the remaining egg and 1 tbsp water. Brush lightly over the tops of the scones. Try not to get any on the sides, as this will prevent the scones from rising. Bake for 12 minutes or until golden brown on top. Transfer to a wire rack. Serve slightly warm with jam and clotted cream.

MY BROTHER NEIL

Fruit Tarts

MAKES 8

275g **plain flour**, plus extra
for dusting
25g **ground almonds**
50g **icing sugar**
½ tsp **salt**
seeds from ½ **vanilla pod** or
1 tsp **vanilla bean paste**
175g **unsalted butter**, chilled and
diced, plus extra for greasing
1 large **egg yolk**
1 tbsp **iced water**

For the pastry cream filling
300ml **whole milk**
4 large **egg yolks**
30g **caster sugar**
1 tbsp **plain flour**
1 tsp **vanilla bean paste**

For the fruit topping
200g **apricot** or **seedless
raspberry jam**, sieved
600g **fresh fruit** (such as
**blueberries, raspberries,
strawberries, cherries**)

These little tarts are perfect for a summer afternoon tea when soft fruits and berries are plentiful and at their best. You can top the tarts them with whatever fruit you fancy, but my favourites are blueberries, strawberries and raspberries.

1. Put the flour, ground almonds, icing sugar and salt together in the bowl of a food processor and pulse to combine. Add the seeds from the vanilla pod or vanilla bean paste and the butter, and pulse until the mixture resembles coarse breadcrumbs. (Alternatively, rub the butter into the flour and vanilla mixture by hand or using a pastry cutter, to resemble coarse breadcrumbs.) Mix the egg yolk and the iced water together, then add this to the mixture. Pulse (or stir) until the mixture just comes together, adding a little more water, little by little, if necessary.

2. Tip onto a lightly floured work surface and knead lightly until uniform. Divide the dough in half and wrap in clingfilm. Chill for at least 30 minutes until ready to use.

3. To make the filling, put the milk into a medium pan over medium–high heat and bring to the boil. Meanwhile, in a medium bowl, whisk the egg yolks, sugar and flour until pale and smooth. Once the milk has come to temperature, slowly pour half over the egg mixture, whisking constantly. Pour the egg mixture back into the pan and put back on the heat. Cook over medium heat, whisking constantly, until thickened. Pour the pastry cream into a bowl and stir in the vanilla bean paste. Press a piece of clingfilm onto the surface to stop a skin forming. Cool and chill.

4. Remove the pastry from the fridge and leave to rest for 10 minutes before rolling out. Lightly grease eight 10cm tart tins with a little butter and set aside. Roll out the pastry on a lightly floured work surface until about 3–4mm thick and cut out eight rounds of pastry about 12.5cm in diameter. Line the prepared tins with the rounds of pastry, trimming away any excess. Line each tart tin with a piece of baking parchment and fill with baking beans or rice. Chill the pastry for 10–15 minutes before baking. Preheat the oven to 180°C (160°C fan oven) mark 4.

5. Bake the pastry shells for 15 minutes, then carefully remove the baking parchment and beans and return to the oven for a further 10–15 minutes or until the pastry is golden. Allow the tarts to cool before removing them from the tins.

6. Warm the jam in a pan over medium heat until dissolved. Fill each tart with a layer of pastry cream. Top each with a little pile of fruit, and brush with a layer of jam. Serve within a few hours of assembling.

138

Chocolate & Ginger Tarts

MAKES 12

- 275g **plain flour**, plus extra for dusting
- 25g **ground almonds**
- 50g **icing sugar**
- ½ tsp **salt**
- 175g **unsalted butter**, cut into small pieces, plus extra for greasing
- 1 large **egg yolk**
- 1 tbsp ice-cold water
- seeds from 1 **vanilla pod**
- 4 pieces **preserved stem ginger** in syrup, drained and finely chopped

For the chocolate ganache
- 225g **dark chocolate** (about 70% cocoa solids), finely chopped
- 185ml **double cream**
- 45g **light brown sugar**
- 40g **unsalted butter**, softened and cut into pieces

These little tarts are pure indulgence and perfect for afternoon tea. They're great if you want to treat someone to something a little bit special. The chocolate and the ginger balance very well and the addition of the light brown sugar tempers the bitterness sometimes associated with dark chocolate.

1. Mix the flour, almonds, icing sugar and salt together in a large bowl, then, using your fingertips, rub in the butter until it resembles coarse uneven breadcrumbs. Mix the egg yolk and 1 tbsp ice-cold water together, and add to the bowl with the vanilla seeds, mixing until the dough just comes together. If necessary, gradually add a little more water until you get the correct consistency. Tip the dough onto a lightly floured work surface and knead lightly until just uniform. Flatten into a disc and wrap in clingfilm. Chill for 30 minutes–1 hour until ready to use.

2. Preheat the oven to 180°C (160°C fan oven) mark 4 and lightly grease a 12-cup muffin pan. Remove the chilled pastry from the fridge and allow to rest at room temperature for 10 minutes. Lightly flour the work surface roll out the pastry to 3–4mm thick. Cut out 12 discs of pastry about 10cm in diameter, and use to line the prepared muffin cups. Line each tart shell with a piece of baking parchment and fill each with a layer of baking beans or rice. Bake for 12–15 minutes, then remove the baking beans and baking parchment, and bake for a further 5–10 minutes or until the tarts are golden. Remove from the oven and allow to cool before filling.

3. To make the ganache, put the chocolate into a medium heatproof bowl and set aside. Put the cream and sugar into a small pan over medium heat and bring just to the boil, remove from the heat and pour over the chocolate. Allow to stand for a couple of minutes before gently stirring together to form a silky smooth ganache. Add the butter and stir to combine.

4. To assemble the tarts, sprinkle the ginger over the base of each tart and top with the chocolate ganache. Allow to set for 1 hour before serving.

TIP

My favourite way to serve these tarts is to decorate them with a small piece of edible gold leaf and a little whipped cream.

140

Caramelised Banana & Passion Fruit Tarts

MAKES 12

500g **all-butter puff pastry**, thawed if frozen
caster sugar, to sprinkle

For the passion fruit curd
175g **caster sugar**
5 large **egg yolks**
80ml sieved **passion fruit purée** (about 5 passion fruit)
100g **unsalted butter**

For the caramelised bananas
3 medium **bananas**
30g **unsalted butter**
30g **light brown sugar**

I had the idea for these little tarts years ago and they have gone through a few different variations, but this is both the simplest and most satisfying one yet. Banana and passion fruit is a wonderful combination and, trust me, these tarts are seriously moreish.

1. To make the passion fruit curd, put the sugar, egg yolks and passion fruit purée into a medium pan over medium heat. Whisk the mixture constantly until the curd thickens and is thick enough to coat the back of a spoon. Take the pan off the heat and add the butter, stirring to combine evenly. Pour the curd into a sterilised jar, then cover, cool and chill until needed.

2. To make the caramelised bananas, first peel and slice the bananas. Put the butter and sugar into a small pan over medium heat and cook until the butter has melted and the sugar has dissolved, and you have a smooth caramel. Cut the banana slices in half and add these to the caramel. Stir to coat evenly, then cook for 2 minutes more. Tip the caramelised banana into a bowl and set aside. Preheat the oven to 200°C (180°C fan oven) mark 6 and lightly grease a standard 12-cup muffin pan.

3. Roll out the puff pastry into a rectangle 1–2mm thick, and cut out 12 rounds 10cm in diameter. Use the pastry rounds to line the prepared muffin pan, then put the pan in the fridge for 15 minutes to let the pastry rest.

4. Prick the base of each tart with a fork, then line each with a piece of baking parchment and fill with baking beans or rice. Bake for 15 minutes, then remove the baking parchment and baking beans and put back in the oven to bake for a further 5–8 minutes or until golden.

5. Put the muffin pan on a wire rack and allow the pastry shells to cool. Remove the cooled shells from the pan and fill each with a layer of the caramelised banana and top with a layer of passion fruit curd. Sprinkle with caster sugar and, using a blowtorch, caramelise the sugar, leaving you with a crème brûlée-like top. (Alternatively, put the tarts under a hot grill until the sugar caramelises; watch carefully as they burn very fast.) These are best served within a couple of hours of assembling.

Cinnamon Rolls

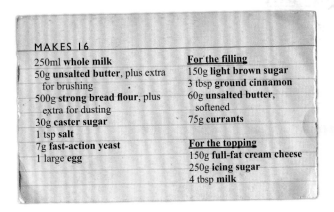

MAKES 16

250ml **whole milk**
50g **unsalted butter**, plus extra for brushing
500g **strong bread flour**, plus extra for dusting
30g **caster sugar**
1 tsp **salt**
7g **fast-action yeast**
1 large **egg**

For the filling
150g **light brown sugar**
3 tbsp **ground cinnamon**
60g **unsalted butter**, softened
75g **currants**

For the topping
150g **full-fat cream cheese**
250g **icing sugar**
4 tbsp **milk**

The smell of freshly baked cinnamon rolls is the thing that dreams are made of – buttery sweet, spicy dreams! Although they take a little time to make, the preparation time is small and the effort is so worth it. When I make these, I always make sure I get one for myself from the centre of the batch, these are softer and, to my mind, just a little bit more scrumptious.

1. Put the milk and butter into a small pan over low heat. Cook until the butter has melted. Allow the mixture to stand until it is just lukewarm. In a large bowl, mix together the flour, sugar, salt and yeast. Add the milk mixture and the egg, and mix to form a soft dough.

2. Lightly flour the work surface and tip the dough onto it. Knead for the dough for 10 minutes or until smooth and elastic. Put the dough in a lightly oiled bowl and cover with clingfilm. Put the bowl into a warm place and leave to rise for 1 hour or until doubled in size. Tip the dough onto a lightly floured work surface and roll the dough into a large rectangle, about 40 × 50cm. Lightly grease a 23 × 33cm high-sided baking tray or brownie pan.

3. To make the filling, mix the light brown sugar and the cinnamon together. Brush the dough with the softened butter and sprinkle the sugar mixture evenly over it. Sprinkle the currants over the dough and then roll it into a tight log starting from the long edge. Trim off the ends of the rolled dough, then slice the dough into 16 equal pieces. Put the rolls into the greased tin and cover with clingfilm. Leave to rise until the rolls have doubled in size, about 45 minutes. Preheat the oven to 180°C (160°C fan oven) mark 4.

4. Mix all the topping ingredients together in a medium bowl until smooth. Brush the buns with a little melted butter and bake them for 30 minutes or until golden. To prevent burning you may need to cover the rolls with foil for the last 5–10 minutes. Allow to cool slightly, then pour the topping onto the rolls and spread it to coat evenly. These are best served warm, so tuck in and enjoy!

TIP

If you want to make these rolls ready for breakfast, you can cover them with clingfilm or a damp tea towel and chill them overnight, once the dough has been rolled and sliced and put into the baking tray ready for the final proving. When ready to bake in the morning, take the rolls out of the fridge about 30 minutes before baking, to bring them to room temperature.

144

Risquits

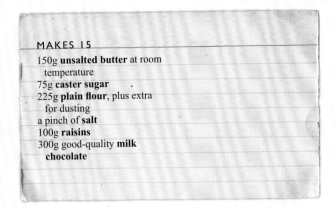

MAKES 15

150g **unsalted butter** at room temperature
75g **caster sugar**
225g **plain flour**, plus extra for dusting
a pinch of **salt**
100g **raisins**
300g good-quality **milk chocolate**

These are total nostalgia for me. They are my version of a chocolate biscuit I sometimes had in my lunchbox when I was in primary school. There was a very well-known TV advert for the treat, and I can still remember the theme tune today. My version uses a buttery shortbread studded with raisins as the base, hence the name risquits: raisin biscuits.

1. Line a baking sheet with baking parchment. Put the butter and sugar into a medium bowl and beat together until smooth and creamy. Add the flour, salt and raisins, and mix together until evenly combined. Tip onto a lightly floured work surface and gently knead together until uniform.

2. Roll out the dough to about 1cm thick. Cut out 15 8 × 3.5cm rectangles and put on the prepared baking sheet. Chill for 30 minutes or until the biscuits are firm. Preheat the oven to 180°C (160°C fan oven) mark 4.

3. Bake for 20–25 minutes or until the edges are golden. Allow to cool on the baking sheet for 10 minutes before transferring to a wire rack to cool completely.

4. To coat the biscuits, have a baking sheet lined with baking parchment ready to use. Melt the chocolate in a heatproof bowl set over a pan of gently simmering water, making sure the base of the bowl doesn't touch the water. Remove from the heat and dip the biscuits in the chocolate, coating them completely. Use a fork to lift them out and put the coated biscuits on the parchment-lined baking sheet to set.

Chocolate-Dipped Flapjacks

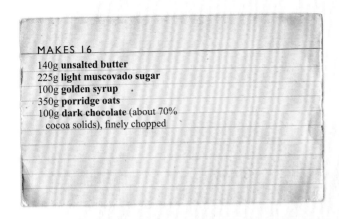

MAKES 16

140g **unsalted butter**
225g **light muscovado sugar**
100g **golden syrup**
350g **porridge oats**
100g **dark chocolate** (about 70% cocoa solids), finely chopped

When I was at primary school I remember being picked up after school by my mum, and sometimes as a treat we would go to the bakery in the village, and this would often be my choice. Chewy oats covered in chocolate made for one very happy seven-year-old.

1. Preheat the oven to 180°C (160°C fan oven) mark 4, and line a 23 × 33cm baking tin with foil or baking parchment. Put the butter, sugar and golden syrup in a large pan over medium heat, and cook until the butter and sugar have melted and the mixture is smooth.

2. Remove from the heat and tip in the oats. Stir until the oats are coated evenly in the sugar mixture. Tip the flapjack mixture into the prepared tin and press firmly into an even layer. Bake for 20–25 minutes or until the edges are starting to turn golden.

3. Allow to cool completely in the tin before lifting the baking parchment and the flapjack out and cutting into squares. Line a baking sheet with baking parchment. Melt the chocolate in a heatproof bowl set over a pan of gently simmering water, making sure the base of the bowl doesn't touch the water. Dip each flapjack into the chocolate, coating half of each piece in chocolate. Set on the baking parchment and chill until the chocolate sets.

Lamingtons

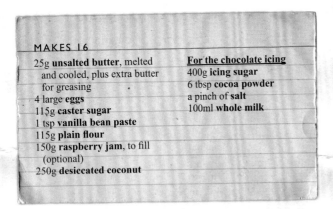

MAKES 16

25g **unsalted butter**, melted
    and cooled, plus extra butter
    for greasing
4 large **eggs**
115g **caster sugar**
1 tsp **vanilla bean paste**
115g **plain flour**
150g **raspberry jam**, to fill
    (optional)
250g **desiccated coconut**

For the chocolate icing
400g **icing sugar**
6 tbsp **cocoa powder**
a pinch of **salt**
100ml **whole milk**

Australia: home to the kangaroo, the
didgeridoo and the delicious Lamington.
It's a simple combination of chocolate,
coconut and sponge cake – just a few
ingredients, but we all know that simple
is sometimes better. These cakes are great
for kids to get involved in making – they
can get messy dipping the cakes into the
chocolate and rolling them in the coconut.

1. Preheat the oven to 180°C (160°C fan oven) mark 4, then grease and line a 20cm square cake tin with baking parchment, greasing the parchment too. Put the eggs, sugar and vanilla paste into a heatproof bowl set over a pan of gently simmering water, making sure the base of the bowl doesn't touch the water. Whisk constantly until the sugar has dissolved and the mixture is just warm to the touch.

2. Remove the bowl from the pan and, using an electric mixer, whisk for 5 minutes on high speed then reduce to medium and whisk for a further 3 minutes. By this stage the mixture should have tripled in volume, and when the whisk is lifted from the bowl it should form a slowly dissolving ribbon.

3. Sift in the flour and gently fold together, making sure all the flour is combined but trying to keep as much volume as possible. Take a large spoonful of the batter and add it to the melted butter, then mix together (this will lighten the butter and help to incorporate it into the batter). Gently fold this into the batter.

4. Pour the batter into the prepared tin and gently level out. Bake for 25 minutes or until risen and golden; and a skewer inserted into the centre of the cake comes out clean. Allow the cake to cool in the tin for 10 minutes before turning out onto a wire rack to cool completely.

5. To make the icing, put the icing sugar, cocoa powder and salt into a medium bowl and mix together. Add the milk and mix until you have a smooth, thin chocolate sauce. Using a serrated knife, slice the cake into 5cm squares.

6. For jam-filled Lamingtons, slice the cakes in half through the centre and sandwich together with a little raspberry jam. Put the coconut on a large, shallow plate. Dip the cake in the chocolate icing to coat it completely. This might be messy work, but it's fun! Once fully coated, roll in the coconut and set on baking parchment to set.

Dulce de Leche Madeleines

MAKES 12

2 large **eggs**
100g **caster sugar**
100g **plain flour**, plus extra
  for dusting
½ tsp **baking powder**
100g **unsalted butter**, melted
  and cooled, plus extra butter
  for greasing

**For the dulce de leche
filling**
400g can **dulce de leche**
¼ tsp **flaked sea salt**

Madeleines should be delicious, but shop-bought ones can often be disappointing, heavy and tasteless. But why buy them when they are super-easy to make? To amp up the flavour even more I have filled them with dulce de leche, a milk-based caramel often used in banoffee pie. Once you have eaten them this way you'll probably never want them plain again!

1. Put the eggs and sugar into a large bowl set over a pan of gently simmering water, and whisk constantly until the sugar dissolves and the egg mixture is warm. Remove the bowl from the pan and, using an electric mixer, whisk on high speed for 5 minutes, reduce the speed to medium and beat for a further 3 minutes.

2. Sift the flour and baking powder over the egg mixture and gently fold together until no streaks of flour remain. Take a large spoonful of the batter and add it to the melted butter, then mix together (this will lighten the butter and help to incorporate it into the batter). Gently fold this into the batter. Cover the bowl with clingfilm and chill for at least 1 hour or up to two days before using.

3. Preheat the oven to 180°C (160°C fan oven) mark 4 and grease a standard 12-cup Madeleine pan, making sure to grease all the ridges. (If you don't have a Madeleine pan you could use a 12-cup muffin pan, although of course the shape will differ.) Dust the pan with flour and tap out any excess. Spoon about 1 tbsp batter into each mould, but don't spread it out; this will happen naturally in the oven. Bake for 12–14 minutes until golden around the edges. Allow to cool in the pan for 5 minutes before turning out onto a wire rack to cool completely.

4. To make the filling, put the dulce de leche and salt into a small pan over medium heat. Stir regularly until the caramel thins out and the salt has dissolved. (This recipe makes more filling then needed, but the extra can be used to pour over ice cream.)

5. Put the filling into a piping bag fitted with a small plain piping tip and press the tip into the end of the Madeleines, squeezing about 1 tsp of the caramel into each.

TIP

Dulce de leche is available in most supermarkets, but is sometimes sold as 'caramel' and stocked with the condensed and evaporated milks.

151

Blueberry & Mango Meringue Bites

MAKES 20-30 MERINGUES

2 large **egg whites**
a pinch of **salt**
100g **caster sugar**

For the filling
1 large **mango**, diced
150g **blueberries**
200ml **double cream**

These dainty meringues are full of the flavour of fresh fruit, with the sweetness of the meringue and the rich cream to hold it all together. I have filled mine with blueberries and mango, but you can fill them with whatever fruit takes your fancy.

1. Preheat oven to 110°C (90°C fan oven) mark ¼ and line a baking sheet with baking parchment. Put the egg whites and salt into a clean, grease-free bowl and, using an electric mixer, whisk until they form stiff peaks. Add the sugar, a spoonful at a time, while continuing to whisk, until all the sugar is fully incorporated and the meringue is glossy and holds stiff peaks.

2. Spoon the meringue into a piping bag fitted with a small star piping tip and pipe circles 4cm in diameter onto the baking parchment. Bake for 1–1½ hours or until dry but still white. Turn off the oven and leave the meringues to cool in the oven.

3. To make the filling, mix the diced mango with the blueberries. Put the cream into a medium bowl and whisk until it holds medium peaks. Add a small amount of cream to each meringue and top with fruit. Serve immediately.

TIP

If you want to make these in advance, you can store them for up to one week, without the filling, in a sealed container and assemble them as required. As soon as you add cream they will slowly start to soften and must be served immediately.

152

Key Lime Cake

SERVES 12

225g **unsalted butter** at room temperature, plus extra for greasing
325g **plain flour**
50g **cornflour**
¼ tsp **salt**
4½ tsp **baking powder**
400g **caster sugar**
5 medium **egg whites**, lightly beaten

2 tsp **vanilla extract**
300ml **buttermilk**

For the filling and frosting
700ml **double cream**
400g **lime curd**
lime zest, to decorate

The sweet-and-sharp filling of key lime pie against the sweet base and the creamy topping is just wonderful! Those flavours can be transformed into an impressive triple-layered cake for a celebration. Instead of finishing it with a frosting or buttercream, it is covered with whipped cream, so like the original pie, this celebration cake is a lot less sweet compared to many others.

1. Preheat the oven to 180°C (160°C fan oven) mark 4, then grease and line three 20cm cake tins with baking parchment, greasing the parchment too. In a medium bowl mix together the flour, cornflour, salt and baking powder, then set aside.

2. Put the butter in a large bowl and, using an electric mixer, beat until light and creamy, about 3–4 minutes. Add the sugar to the butter and beat until light and fluffy, about 5 minutes. Add the egg whites and vanilla, a little at a time, beating until fully combined before adding more. With the mixer on low, sift in the flour mixture in three additions, alternating with the buttermilk, starting and finishing with the flour, beating until just combined. Divide equally among the prepared tins and bake for 30 minutes or until the cake springs back when lightly touched; a skewer inserted into the cakes should come out clean. Cool in the tins for 10 minutes before turning out onto a wire rack to cool completely.

3. To assemble the cake, whisk the cream to medium-firm peaks and then put a small amount onto a cardboard cake round or serving plate. Put the first cake layer onto the board – the cream will keep it in place. Fill a piping bag fitted with a large plain piping tip with a quarter of the cream. Pipe a border around the edge of the first cake layer – this will act as a dam to stop the lime curd from leaking.

4. Beat the lime curd with a small spatula to loosen it, then spread an even layer across the cake. Using the piping bag, cover the curd with a layer of cream. Top with the second cake layer and repeat. Put the final cake layer on top and use the remaining cream to cover the sides and top of the cake. My favourite way to decorate the cake is to keep it very simple and just grate a little lime zest over the top.

Raspberry Ripple Choux Buns

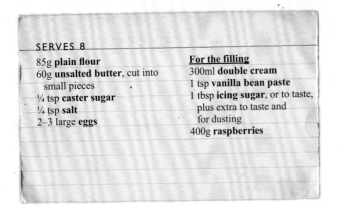

SERVES 8

85g **plain flour**
60g **unsalted butter**, cut into
  small pieces
¼ tsp **caster sugar**
¼ tsp **salt**
2–3 large **eggs**

For the filling

300ml **double cream**
1 tsp **vanilla bean paste**
1 tbsp **icing sugar**, or to taste,
  plus extra to taste and
  for dusting
400g **raspberries**

Raspberry and cream is a wonderful pairing: the tartness of the berries along with the creaminess of the double cream. Fill a choux bun with the two and you have a lovely little treat that is also a bit lighter if you fancy something slightly less calorific than a big slice of cake.

1. Preheat the oven to 200°C (180°C fan oven) mark 6, and line two baking sheets with baking parchment. Sift the flour onto a sheet of greaseproof paper. Put the butter, sugar, salt and 140ml water into a medium pan over medium–high heat and bring to a rolling boil. Take off the heat and tip in the flour. Using a wooden spoon, beat to combine. Put back on the heat and beat the dough for a few minutes or until the dough comes away from the sides of the pan.

2. Tip the dough into a medium bowl and beat vigorously until no longer steaming. Beat in the eggs, one at a time – you may not need them all; check the consistency of the dough after each addition. It should be smooth and shiny and will fall from the wooden spoon forming a V-shaped ribbon. If it looks almost right after 2 eggs, just add a little of the third and test again. Put the dough into a piping bag fitted with a plain piping tube and pipe into rounds on the prepared baking sheet about 2.5 cm in diameter. Using a finger dipped in water, gently tap any peaks down.

3. Bake for 20–25 minutes or until risen and golden brown. Remove the baking sheet from the oven and, using a sharp knife, make a hole in the base of each choux bun. Turn the heat off and put the choux buns back into the oven, base up, for 10 minutes; this will help keep the buns crisp.

4. To make the filling, put the cream, vanilla paste and icing sugar into a large bowl and whisk until the cream holds medium–stiff peaks. In a small bowl, mash half the raspberries using the back of a fork and add a little icing sugar, just to sweeten the mixture a little. Fold this mixture into the cream with the remaining raspberries. Slice the choux buns in half and fill with the cream mixture. Dust with a little icing sugar to serve.

Pistachio French Crullers

MAKES 12

	For the glaze and topping
85g **plain flour**	100g **icing sugar**
60g **unsalted butter**, diced	1 tbsp **clear honey**
½ tsp **caster sugar**	1–2 tbsp **milk**
¼ tsp **salt**	125g **pistachios**, shelled
2–3 large **eggs**	and finely chopped
vegetable oil, for deep-frying	

French crullers are a type of doughnut made with choux pastry instead of the usual yeasted dough or cake batter. In my opinion, these are probably the easiest doughnuts to make. Using choux pastry makes them very light and rather moreish. I have topped the doughnuts with pistachios, but if you want a more classic cruller, just use the glaze.

1. Line two baking sheets with baking parchment and set aside. Sift the flour onto a sheet of greaseproof paper. Put the butter, sugar, salt and 140ml water into a medium pan over medium–high heat and bring to a rolling boil. Take off the heat and tip in the flour. Using a wooden spoon, beat to just combine. Put back over medium heat and beat the dough for a few minutes or until it comes away from the sides of the pan and leaves a film of dough on the base of the pan.

2. Tip the dough into a medium bowl and beat vigorously until no longer steaming. Beat in the eggs, one at a time – you may not need them all; check the consistency of the dough after each addition. It should be smooth and shiny and will fall from the wooden spoon forming a V-shaped ribbon, however it shouldn't be runny, it should be fairly thick. If it looks almost right after 2 eggs, just add a little of the third and test again.

3. Put the dough into a piping bag fitted with a large star piping tip and pipe 12 rings of dough onto the prepared baking sheets. Freeze the sheets for 1 hour or until the rings of dough can be peeled off the baking parchment.

4. Make the glaze by mixing the icing sugar, honey and enough milk to make a thick but pourable glaze. Pour the vegetable oil into a large heavy-based pan up to a depth of 5cm and heat to 180–190°C over medium–high heat. When ready to fry the doughnuts, have a baking sheet lined with kitchen paper ready to drain the excess oil.

5. Put one or two doughnuts into the oil and fry for a few minutes on each side until browned. Use a slotted spoon to remove the doughnuts from the oil and put them on the kitchen paper. Fry the remaining doughnuts. While they are still warm, dip them in the glaze and then into the pistachios.

TIP

These are best served as fresh as possible and definitely on the day of making.

156

Jammy Dodgers

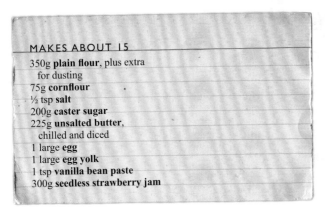

MAKES ABOUT 15

350g **plain flour**, plus extra
  for dusting
75g **cornflour**
½ tsp **salt**
200g **caster sugar**
225g **unsalted butter**,
  chilled and diced
1 large **egg**
1 large **egg yolk**
1 tsp **vanilla bean paste**
300g **seedless strawberry jam**

Trying to recreate biscuits and cookies from my childhood for this book was a lot of fun - it brought back lots of memories. These may seem simple - just a vanilla cookie with jam - but trying to get the filling to have the same slight chew like the original cookies was a little tricky. Then an idea came to me - and I found that a blowtorch does a pretty good job. (If you don't have a blowtorch they are still delicious without using one.)

1.   Line two baking sheets with baking parchment. Put the flour, cornflour, salt and sugar in the bowl of a food processor and pulse to combine. Add the butter and pulse until the mixture resembles coarse breadcrumbs. (Alternatively, rub the butter into the flour mixture by hand or using a pastry cutter, to resemble coarse breadcrumbs.) Add the egg, yolk and vanilla paste, and pulse (or stir) until the mixture just comes together.

2.   Tip onto a lightly floured work surface and gently knead together until uniform. Divide the dough in half and wrap in clingfilm, then chill for about 1 hour.

3.   Working with one half of the dough at a time, roll out to a thickness of 3–4mm. Cut out rounds using a 7cm cookie cutter. Re-roll the scraps to cut out more biscuits. Using a 2cm round cutter, remove a hole from the centre of half the rounds. Lift the cookies off the surface with a spatula and put onto the prepared baking sheets, then chill for 15–20 minutes. Preheat the oven to 180°C (160°C fan oven) mark 4.

4.   Bake for 13–15 minutes or until the edges turn golden. Transfer to a wire rack to cool slightly. Add a teaspoonful of jam to each base cookie, and spread it almost to the edge. To give the jam a slight chew, use a blowtorch to gently heat the jam, until it is bubbling a little. Add a ring cookie and lightly press together. Allow to cool fully before serving.

Custard Creams

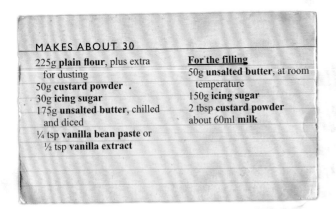

MAKES ABOUT 30

225g **plain flour**, plus extra for dusting	**For the filling**
50g **custard powder**	50g **unsalted butter**, at room temperature
30g **icing sugar**	150g **icing sugar**
175g **unsalted butter**, chilled and diced	2 tbsp **custard powder**
¼ tsp **vanilla bean paste** or ½ tsp **vanilla extract**	about 60ml **milk**

These sandwiched cream biscuits are a British classic, and I love them. Some might find them a bit old-fashioned, but I think they are due for a revival. Simple custard-flavoured biscuits filled with a super-simple custard-tasting buttercream - they are crumbly and light, and perfect with a cup of tea.

1.   Line a baking sheet with baking parchment. Put the flour, custard powder and icing sugar into the bowl of a food processor and pulse to combine. Add the butter and vanilla, and pulse until the mixture begins to come together. If the butter is very cold you may need to knead it together into a mass by hand. (Alternatively, put

158

the dry ingredients into a bowl and rub in the butter by hand or using a pastry cutter, to resemble fine crumbs. Stir in the vanilla.) Tip the mixture onto the work surface and bring it together into a uniform mass. Wrap in clingfilm and chill for 30 minutes.

2. Remove the dough from the fridge and allow it to rest for 10 minutes at room temperature. Put the dough on a lightly floured work surface and roll to a thickness of 3–4mm. Cut out small rounds using a 3cm cookie cutter and prick in the centre with a fork. Re-roll the scraps to cut out more biscuits. Put on the baking sheet and chill for 15 minutes or until firm. Preheat the oven to 180°C (160°C fan oven) mark 4.

3. Bake the biscuits for 10 minutes or until just starting to colour around the edges. Allow the biscuits to cool on the baking sheet for 5 minutes before transferring to a wire rack to cool completely.

4. To make the filling, beat the butter using an electric mixer until light and creamy, about 5 minutes, then slowly incorporate the icing sugar, custard powder and 60ml milk. Once fully combined, beat on high speed until smooth and fluffy. The mixture will be stiffer than a cake frosting; if you prefer something a little easier to work with you can add a little more milk.

5. Put the buttercream into a piping bag fitted with a small plain piping tube and pipe onto half the biscuits, then sandwich them together with a second biscuit. (If you prefer, you can use a knife to spread the filling onto the biscuits instead of piping, but be careful, because these biscuits are very fragile.)

Digestives

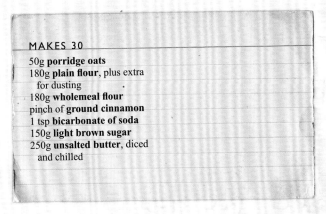

MAKES 30

50g **porridge oats**
180g **plain flour**, plus extra for dusting
180g **wholemeal flour**
pinch of **ground cinnamon**
1 tsp **bicarbonate of soda**
150g **light brown sugar**
250g **unsalted butter**, diced and chilled

What better biscuit to dunk in a cup of tea than a classic digestive. Not too sweet, nice and crisp and, of course, delicious. My favourite way to eat these is with a little butter and a wedge of mature Cheddar – wonderful stuff!

1. Line two baking trays with baking parchment. Put the oats in the bowl of a food processor and pulse until finely ground. Add the flours, cinnamon, bicarbonate of soda and sugar, and pulse to combine. Add the butter and pulse until the mixture just starts to come together. (Alternatively, use a blender to grind the oats, then tip into a bowl with the dry ingredients. Rub the butter into the dry ingredients by hand or using a pastry cutter, to resemble fine crumbs, then bring it together with your hands.)

2. Tip the dough onto the work surface and knead gently until smooth and uniform. Flatten the dough into a disc and wrap in clingfilm. Chill the dough in the fridge for at least 30 minutes before using. If chilled for longer, allow it to come to room temperature before rolling out.

3. Put the dough onto a lightly floured work surface and roll to a thickness of 4–5mm. Cut out small rounds using a 7cm round cutter. Re-roll the scraps to cut out more biscuits. Put onto the prepared baking sheets and chill for 20–30 minutes. Preheat the oven to 180°C (160°C fan oven) mark 4.

4. Bake for 15 minutes or until golden and the edges are lightly browned. Transfer to a wire rack to cool completely. These biscuits will keep for at least three days stored in an airtight sealed container.

Bourbons

MAKES ABOUT 30

225g **plain flour**, plus extra for dusting	**For the chocolate ganache filling**
50g **cocoa powder**	110g **dark chocolate** (about 70% cocoa solids), finely chopped
75g **icing sugar**	
¼ tsp **salt**	120ml **double cream**
180g **unsalted butter**, chilled	30g **light brown sugar**
1 large **egg**	25g **unsalted butter** at room temperature, cut into small pieces

Most of the biscuits in this chapter were taken straight from my childhood, but instead of just recreating the bourbon as I remember I have made a slightly more grown-up version. The biscuit uses something more akin to a pastry dough, and because of this it is lighter and more flaky than the original. I have also filled it with ganache rather than buttercream to make the biscuits less like the childhood ones and more fitting to serve with a cup of strong coffee.

1. Line two baking sheets with baking parchment. Put the flour, cocoa powder, icing sugar and salt into the bowl of a food processor and pulse to combine. Add the butter and pulse until the mixture resembles coarse breadcrumbs. (Alternatively, rub the butter into the flour mixture by hand or using a pastry cutter, to resemble coarse breadcrumbs.) Add the egg and pulse (or stir) until the mixture just begins to come together.

2. Tip the mixture onto a lightly floured work surface and lightly knead together until uniform. Wrap in clingfilm and chill for about 1 hour.

3. Remove the dough from the fridge and allow to stand for a few minutes before rolling. Dust the work surface with a little flour and roll out the dough until it is about 2mm thick. Using a knife or pizza cutter, cut out rectangles of dough about 6 × 3cm and transfer to the prepared baking sheets. Re-roll the scraps to cut out more biscuits.

4. Use a fork to prick the biscuits a few times, this will prevent them from rising. Put the trays into the fridge for 15–20 minutes or until the pastry is firm. Preheat the oven to 180°C (160°C fan oven) mark 4.

5. Bake the biscuits for 20–25 minutes or until crisp and browning slightly around the edges. Transfer to a wire rack to cool completely before filling.

6. To make the ganache, put the chocolate into a medium heatproof bowl and set aside. Put the cream and sugar into a medium pan over medium heat and bring just to the boil, remove from the heat and pour over the chocolate. Allow to stand for a couple of minutes before stirring together to form a silky smooth ganache.

7. Add the butter and stir to combine. Allow the ganache to stand until it has thickened enough to pipe. Fill a piping bag fitted with a small plain piping tube and pipe onto half the cookies. (Alternatively, you can spoon on the ganache.) Sandwich together with a second cookie and allow the ganache to fully set before serving.

CHAPTER FOUR: AFTERNOON TEA & PICNICS

Coconut Macaroon Sandwiches

5 large **egg whites**
a pinch of **salt**
1 tsp **vanilla extract**
430g **desiccated coconut**
250g **caster sugar**
150g **raspberry** or
   strawberry jam

At my afternoon tea I don't serve real sandwiches. My tea is all about the sweet stuff, so these macaroons are the 'savoury' course, filled with jam and sliced to look like dainty finger sandwiches.

1. Preheat the oven to 170°C (150°C fan oven) mark 3 and grease a 20cm square cake tin. Line with a strip of baking parchment, leaving a 5cm overhang (so that you can remove the macaroon easily) and set aside. Put the egg whites, salt and vanilla extract into a clean, grease-free bowl and whisk until frothy. Add the coconut and caster sugar, and mix with a wooden spoon until very well combined.

2. Take half the macaroon mixture and press it into the prepared tin, using a spoon to ensure an even, tightly packed layer. Spread the jam evenly over the base layer of coconut and then put spoonfuls of the macaroon mixture across the jam. Use a spoon to level the mixture out, sealing in the jam.

3. Bake for 40 minutes or until the top of the macaroon is a light golden colour. Allow to cool completely in the tin, and then chill for 1 hour. This will firm up the macaroon a little and make it easier to remove and cut.

4. Lift out the macaroon and put onto a cutting board. Using a serrated knife, cut into squares or triangles to look like sandwiches.

Templates

Gingerbread House

These are the templates for the Gingerbread House on page 128. To use, trace over these outlines and cut out your own templates. Place your templates onto the rolled out dough and use a knife or pizza wheel to cut the pieces out.

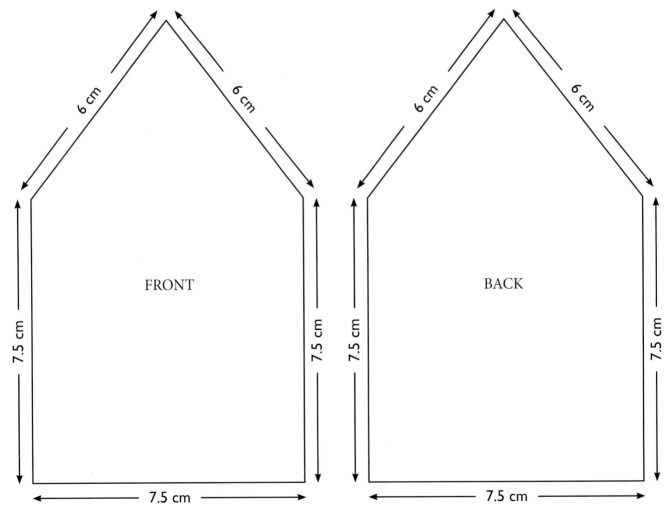

FRONT

6 cm   6 cm

7.5 cm   7.5 cm

7.5 cm

BACK

6 cm   6 cm

7.5 cm   7.5 cm

7.5 cm

7.5 cm

10 cm

ROOF

7.5 cm

10 cm

ROOF

7.5 cm

10 cm

WALL

7.5 cm

10 cm

WALL

Wedding Cake Cookies

This is the template for the Wedding Cake Cookies on page 62. Instead of buying a cookie cutter, you can trace this design and use it as a template to cut out the cookies.

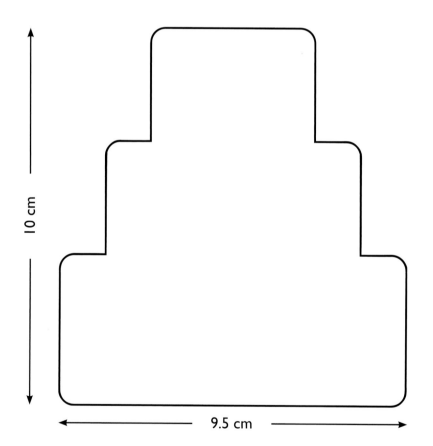

10 cm

9.5 cm

168

MATT'S PARENTS ON THEIR WEDDING DAY

Resources

CAKES, COOKIES AND CRAFTS SHOP

www.cakescookiesandcraftsshop.co.uk

Extensive online shop with a wide selection of bakeware and cake decoration supplies, including cake boards, doweling rods, ribbon, sugarpaste etc for wedding and celebration cakes.

SQUIRES KITCHEN

www.squires-shop.com

Large range of products for cake decorating and baking including edible gold.

JOHN LEWIS

www.johnlewis.com

Supplier of small electrical appliances including Kitchenaid Stand Mixers.

NISBETS

www.nisbets.com

Specialist restaurant supply shop who stock good-quality bakeware including baking sheets and terrine moulds.

LAKELAND

www.lakeland.co.uk

Large range of general cookware and bakeware.

POLYSTYRENE CONES

You can buy small polystyrene cones at craft shops such as: **www.hobbycraft.co.uk** but if you need a larger cone like the one I used for my macaron tower then you can get custom-sized cones from **www.grahamsweet.com.**

EDIBLE FLOWERS

www.waitrose.com

www.scotherbs.co.uk

www.firstleaf.co.uk

It is advisable to get your edible flowers from a supplier who can guarantee that the flowers didn't come into contact with pesticides.

BUNDT/BUNDLETTE PANS

I prefer those made by Nordic Ware and they are available at most department stores and all good cookshops including the ones mentioned above.

Index

Thank you

First and foremost my thanks go to Matt – you put up with me for months whilst I made a mess of our kitchen and constantly fed you cake. Thanks for being a huge support and for calming me down when I got stressed. I love you very much.

Thank you to everyone in my family who dug into the photo albums looking for lots of old pictures of family occasions – it was great to see them and to remember forgotten events.

Thanks to everyone at Kyle Books, especially Kyle and Catharine. I really think this is a beautiful book and it's down to your continued support that I got to write it.

Working on the photography was so much fun and I love the results. Georgia, you did an amazing job, I couldn't be happier – thanks for a fun-filled few weeks. Anna and Emily, thank you for making me laugh and making my food look delicious – working with you both was brilliant. Anita, you took my idea and ran away with it. I am thrilled with the design – thank you so much.

And thank you to everyone who bought my first book and for picking up this one. I love writing the books and I hope you enjoy baking from them.

Happy Baking!

Edd

MY WONDERFUL GRANDPARENTS